KU-324-840

# CONTENTS

## WHAT'S IN YOUR GUIDEBOOK?

**Independent authors** Impartial up-to-date information from our travel experts who meticulously source local knowledge.

**Experience** Thomas Cook's 165 years in the travel industry and guidebook publishing enriches every word with expertise you can trust.

**Travel know-how** Thomas Cook has thousands of staff working around the globe, all living and breathing travel.

**Editors** Travel-publishing professionals, pulling everything together to craft a perfect blend of words, pictures, maps and design.

**You, the traveller** We deliver a practical, no-nonsense approach to information, geared to how you really use it.

### ABOUT THE AUTHOR

Katerina Roberts is a British travel writer based in Mauritius. She specialises in the islands of the Indian Ocean region and has produced guides on Mauritius, Seychelles, Réunion, Rodrigues and Sri Lanka. She also contributes travel articles to various media and is a member of Writers and Photographers Unlimited (W www.wpu.org.uk) and Travel Writers UK (W www.travelwriters.co.uk).

◗ *The beach at Balaclava*

# INTRODUCTION
Getting to know Mauritius

Rodrigues Island

Île aux Serpents

Île Ronde

Île Plate

Îlot Gabriel

Coin de Mire

Cap Malheureux

Pointe Bernache

Île d'Ambre

Pointe de
Roches Noires

Poste Lafayette

Grand
Gaube

Goodlands

Roches
Noires

Pereybère

A5

Grand
Baie

M1

Triolet

L'Aventure du Sucre

Pamplemousses

Pamplemousses
Botanic Gardens

A2

Pointe aux
Cannoniers

Trou aux
Biches

Pointe aux
Piments

Balaclava

Indian Ocean

**Mauritius**

0        5 km

0        3 miles

City

Large Town

Small Town

POI

Motorway

Main Road

Minor Road

Airport

N

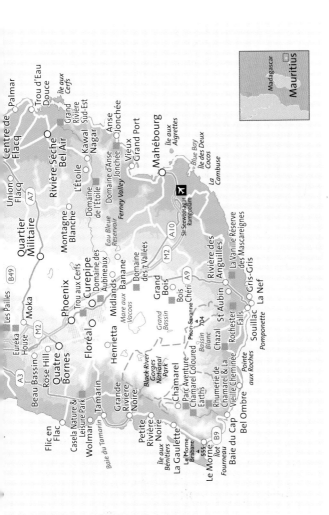

# Getting to know Mauritius

Mauritius, its sister island Rodrigues and the French island of Réunion are known collectively as the Mascarenes. Mauritius, the second largest of the group, is about the same size as Surrey and is 800 km (500 miles) east of Madagascar. Lying 9,650 km (6,000 miles) from Europe in the southwestern Indian Ocean, this holiday island lures thousands of visitors to its shores each year.

And what shores! This beautiful island rose from the sea some 8 million years ago in a series of underwater volcanic eruptions, leaving white beaches and turquoise lagoons protected by virtually unbroken coral reefs. With its pocket-sized mountains, emerald-green landscapes, mysterious gorges, tumbling waterfalls and a welcoming people, Mauritius appeals to fun-loving singles, couples and families alike.

The Dutch arrived in 1598 at an uninhabited island and named it Mauritius, after Prince Maurice of Nassau. They never settled, leaving it to be colonised by the French, who called it *Île de France* in 1710, and the British a hundred years later who renamed it Mauritius. Independence came in 1968 and today Mauritius is one of the safest destinations in the region thanks to a low crime rate, stable economy and democratic government.

The 1.2 million inhabitants are mostly the descendants of African and Malagasy slaves, who worked on sugar plantations when the island was under French rule, and Indian immigrants brought in by the British as indentured labourers when slavery was abolished. There are smaller communities of Chinese and white Europeans of French origin. Each community retains its identity while respecting each other's cultural roots and traditions, yet they're all united as Mauritians and many converse in Creole, a sort of pidgin French. In spite of English being the official language, you'll hear French, Bhojpuri, Hindi and other less familiar languages, witness a plethora of cultural and religious festivals and taste a cuisine that is as diverse as the people.

Mauritius offers far more than your average beach holiday with luxurious hotels to pamper you throughout your stay. Out and about,

INTRODUCTION

whether it's walking with lions at Casela Nature and Leisure Park, hiking in the Black River Gorges, combining culture, history and shopping in Port Louis or a trip to remote Rodrigues, you'll find surprises every step of the way. Mauritius is very much a daytime destination, with the range of exciting activities, from big game fishing and kitesurfing to cruising and dolphin-watching easily compensating for the quieter nightlife. With so much packed into a tiny island you'll never be bored. It's one of the reasons why so many visitors return.

🔺 *Sunset on the horizon at Balaclava*

# THE BEST OF MAURITIUS

Whether you are after sunshine, surf, lush landscapes or cultural attractions, there are lots of fun things to see and do on this beautiful island. Mauritius offers plenty of relaxation and adventure for all.

## TOP 10 ATTRACTIONS

- **Dive, snorkel, windsurf or play around in boats** in calm lagoons. Sunbathe on the beaches of **Balaclava**, **Trou aux Biches** (see pages 49–52), **Mon Choisy** (see page 17), **Belle Mare** (see page 27) and **Flic en Flac** (see page 43).

- **Visit the world-famous Sir Seewoosagur Ramgoolam Botanic Gardens** and spend a morning discovering beautiful flora and fauna (see pages 53–4).

- **Play golf**, taking your pick from seven 18-hole and four 9-hole golf courses set in breathtaking locations (see pages 103–4).

- **Follow the Tea Route**, visiting colonial houses for tea-tasting and marvelling at the remote south coast (see page 78).

- **Cruise along the coast**, picnic on offshore islands (see page 19) or try your hand at big-game fishing (see page 17).

- **Walk in the wild with lions and cheetahs** in the savanna landscapes of Casela Nature and Leisure Park and find out what makes these big cats tick (see page 44).

- **Explore the Black River Gorges** by taking a hike or drive through this national park, home to misty mountains and forests (see page 82).

- **Visit the island of Rodrigues** to see giant tortoises, colonies of seabirds and a fabulous lagoon dotted with islets (see pages 57–62).

- **Discover Port Louis**, the buzzing capital for markets, museums and shopping (see pages 67–74).

- **Take a helicopter tour** to view the glorious lagoons, coastlines and extinct volcanic craters (see page 38).

*Lush vegetation in the Sir Seewoosagur Ramgoolam Botanic Gardens*

## SYMBOLS KEY

The following symbols are used throughout this book:

---

**③** address  **☎** telephone  **⑦** fax  **⑩** website address  **⑨** email
**⑤** opening times  **❶** important

---

The following symbols are used on the maps:

**𝒊** information office

**✉** post office

**▣** shopping

**✈** airport

**✚** hospital

**⬡** police station

**🚌** bus station

**✝** church

○ city

○ large town

○ small town

▦ point of interest

═ motorway

— main road

minor road

**❶** numbers denote featured cafés, restaurants & evening venues
venues in the same area may share the same number

## RESTAURANT CATEGORIES

The symbol after the name of each restaurant listed in this guide
indicates the price of a typical three-course meal without drinks
for one person:

£ under R400   ££ R400–R800   £££ over R800

**◆** *The beach at Mon Choisy*

# RESORTS
Places under the sun

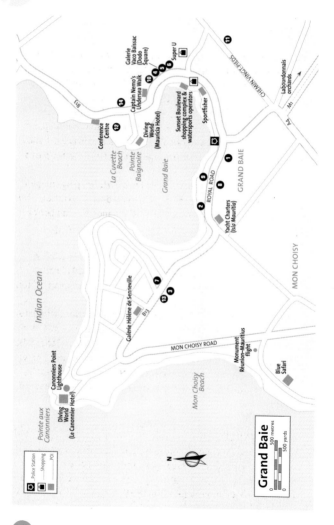

Grand Baie

14

# Grand Baie

Grand Baie, on the northwest tip of Mauritius, is strung along a deep wide bay sprinkled with small fishing boats, catamarans and colourful pleasure craft. What started out as a small fishing village in the 1970s has developed into a full-blown holiday resort with an easy-going international vibe appealing to couples, families and children. There's accommodation to suit all budgets, from simple guesthouses to grand hotels, and all the amenities you would expect in a thriving resort, such as medical and dental services and a large modern supermarket, plus a regular bus service and plenty of taxis.

Bang in the centre of Grand Baie, near the smart shopping complex of Sunset Boulevard, tour operators organise island-wide excursions, fun days at sea or picnics and barbecues on nearby islands. You can book a catamaran trip, explore the deep in a mini submarine, go diving, parasailing or waterskiing, or just find a quiet beach.

Grand Baie is also one of the best places for nightlife, especially on Friday and Saturday, when nightclubs and bars attract locals from all over the island. Midweek there are plenty of cafés, restaurants and shops to explore.

To the west of Grand Baie is the quiet residential headland of **Pointe aux Canonniers**. The French used the low cliffs as a garrison in the 19th century and under the British it became a quarantine station. Today it is dominated by Le Canonnier Hotel, from where there are stunning views of the wedge-shaped island of Coin de Mire. A little way further south, through an avenue of flamboyant trees, is the gorgeous public beach of **Mon Choisy**.

## GETTING ABOUT
Grand Baie has few proper pavements and poor street lighting. If you find yourself forced to walk on to the road, watch out carefully for traffic and other obstacles. It's a good idea to wear comfortable shoes and carry a torch with you at night.

## BEACHES

As picturesque as Grand Baie is, the proliferation of fishing and pleasure boats bobbing in shallow waters means it isn't an ideal place to swim. However, it's pleasant enough gazing across the bay from one of the waterside cafés near Sunset Boulevard, and the privately maintained beaches in front of the hotels are superb.

Beyond the rocky northern tip of the bay the fine public beach, **La Cuvette**, has changing rooms, toilets, showers, a parking area and snack kiosks. Black basalt rocks frame the smooth white sands here and the sea is ideal for swimming and snorkelling. Beyond the rocks you can swim up to the beach fronting the prestigious Royal Palm Hotel, where sunbeds are reserved for guests.

⬣ *Relax in comfort at the water's edge*

Three other beaches hug the headland at **Pointe aux Canonniers** and are used mainly by guests of Le Canonnier Hotel. You can walk and swim here, or take a picnic, but you are not allowed to use the hotel facilities.

For a real fun day out rubbing shoulders with the locals you can't do better than to head for the public beach at **Mon Choisy**. Hemmed in by a distant coral reef, this 2-km (1-mile) crescent of brilliant white sands and azure waters is a pure slice of paradise. Behind the beach a deep forest of casuarina trees provides shade with parking, toilets, food stalls and locals on hand to take you out in a glass-bottom boat. At weekends and on public holidays it can get very crowded so be prepared to share your space with large family groups, some of whom camp overnight.

An odd-looking white monument on the edge of the grassy football ground nearby marks the landing of the first flight from the island of Réunion to Mauritius in 1933. These days local football teams use the grounds, which are also the finishing line of the 100-km (62-mile) cycling tour held in October when hundreds of participants race across the island. At the southern end of Mon Choisy, colourful statues of Hindu gods and shrines attract worshippers, especially at Ganga Asnan in November, an important water purification ritual in the Hindu calendar.

## THINGS TO SEE & DO

### Big game fishing
**Sportfisher** are specialists in half- and full-day big-game-fishing charters. Soft drinks and beer are included, but it's wise to bring your lunch as this is not provided.
ⓐ Sunset Boulevard ⓣ 263 8358 ⓦ www.sportfisher.com ⓔ sportfisher@orange.mu ⓛ 09.00–17.00 Mon–Sat, closed Sun & public holidays
❶ Reservations essential

### Coastal cruise
Take a leisurely cruise along the northwest coast with the serenading crew of the *Isla Mauritia*. Yacht Charters' 19th-century schooner drops

anchor at Tombeau Bay where lunch is provided. Cool off with a swim or go snorkelling.

ⓐ Royal Road, Grand Baie ❶ 263 8395 Ⓦ www.isla-mauritia.com

### Scuba-diving
**Diving World** has multilingual instructors who provide all the usual PADI-approved packages. It also operates from Le Canonnier and Victoria hotels.

ⓐ Mauricia Hotel, Grand Baie ❶ 263 1225, 250 1093 ⓔ divwor@intnet.mu
🕒 09.00–17.00 Mon–Sat, closed Sun & public holidays

### Submarine trip
Marvel at marine life without getting your hair wet in the safety of a **Blue Safari** submarine. Or go for the adrenalin-rush aboard an underwater motor scooter with a guide as your driver!

ⓐ Royal Road, Grand Baie ❶ 263 3333 Ⓦ www.blue-safari.com
ⓔ bluesaf@intnet.mu 🕒 09.00–17.00 Mon–Sat, closed Sun and public holidays ❶ Booking recommended

🔺 *Château de Labourdonnais*

## Undersea walk

Don a helmet at **Captain Nemo's Undersea Walk** and go on a guided walkabout amid coral gardens on the seabed where you get to hand feed an array of different fish.

ⓐ Royal Road, Grand Baie ⓣ 263 7819 ⓛ 09.00–15.00 Mon–Sat, closed Sun

## Watersports

For parasailing, waterskiing, glass-bottom boat and speedboat tours, and trips aboard the semi-submersible *Le Nessée* or the Blue Safari submarine (see opposite) to view Grand Baie's spectacular coral reefs, contact **Ebrahim Travel & Tours**.

ⓐ Royal Road, Grand Baie next to the Mauritius Commercial Bank ⓣ 269 0272 ⓔ gbccar@intnet.mu

## EXCURSIONS FROM GRAND BAIE
### Château Labourdonnais

This beautifully restored Creole mansion (the ancestral home of the Wiehe family) dating from 1859 contains period furniture, sculptures by Michaelangelo and portraits reflecting the colonial lifestyle of an agricultural estate. The spacious grounds boast tropical orchards, a distillery, tortoise park, shop, restaurant and a bar offering free rum tastings.

ⓐ Mapou, off the M1 Motorway ⓣ 266 9533 ⓦ www.unchateau danslanature.com ⓛ 09.00–17.00 daily ❶ Admission charge

## Offshore islands

Operating out of Grand Baie, there are many tour operators offering excursions to the offshore islands. Visit Gabriel, Plate and Ambre in the north for swimming and barbecues, Île aux Bénitiers (see page 45) in the southwest for dolphin-watching and Île aux Cerfs (see page 75) in the east for sandy beaches and watersports. Specialist tour operators are all on Royal Road, the coast road in Grand Baie:

**Ebrahim Travel and Tours** ⓣ 421 1597, 269 0272 ⓔ gbccar@intnet.mu

**Grand Bay Travel and Tours** ☎ 265 5261 ⓦ www.gbtt.com
ⓔ resa.gbtt@intnet.mu
**Northview Tours** ☎ 263 5023 ⓔ northview@intnet.mu

## TAKING A BREAK

**Café Muller £** ❶   Bijou coffee shop with tables set around a flower-filled courtyard. The German owner serves up the best cappuccino in town and home-made cakes. Try the gut-busting buffet brunch on Saturday for imaginative dishes using local produce. ⓐ Royal Road, Grand Baie ☎ 263 5230 ⓛ 09.00–17.00 Mon–Sat, closed Sun ❶ Booking essential for the buffet brunch

**Chez Rams aka Coolen ££** ❷   Popular with expats and locals, the menu is traditional Creole and international with a French twist. Simple rustic décor and lots of atmosphere. ⓐ Royal Road, Grand Baie ☎ 263 8569 ⓛ 10.30–14.00, 17.30–22.30 Mon & Tues, Thur–Sun, closed Wed

⬥ *The* Isla Mauritia

**La Cigale ££** ❸ Cosy French-run pizzeria with outdoor tables overlooking the road. ⓐ Royal Road, Pointe aux Canonniers ❶ 263 0913 ⏱ 12.00–14.00, 17.30–22.30 daily

**Don Camillo ££** ❹ Head to this elegant restaurant for generous portions of pizza, pasta, meat, seafood and vegetarian fare. Try the *calzone* or go for the seafood pancake, washed down with wine or local beer. ⓐ Royal Road, Grand Baie, next to the petrol station ❶ 263 8540 ⏱ 12.00–15.00, 19.00–23.00 Mon–Sat, 18.30–23.00 Sun

**Malibu Spur ££** ❺ This popular South African franchise turns out the best steaks in the north. ⓐ Royal Road, Grand Baie ❶ 263 6419 ⓔ malibuspur@live.co.za ⏱ 09.00–23.00 daily

**La Pagode ££** ❻ Red lanterns, gold décor and a numbered menu of the usual Chinese favourites of wontons, chicken and sweetcorn soup, meat, vegetable and fish dishes. ⓐ Royal Road, Grand Baie ❶ 263 8733 ⏱ 10.30–15.00, 18.00–22.30 daily

**Patch 'n Parrot ££** ❼ Find a TV sports screen and great pub grub in this popular bar set in pretty gardens. ⓐ Royal Road, Pointe aux Canonniers ❶ 269 0374 ⓔ patchnparrotpub@gmail.com ⏱ 12.00–24.00 Fri–Sun, 16.00–24.00 Mon, Wed & Thur, closed Tues

**Thaifoon ££** ❽ First-floor eatery decked in Buddhas, with helpful staff to steer you through an exciting selection of Thai treats. ⓐ Corner of Topize and Royal Road, Grand Baie ❶ 269 1110 ⓦ http://thaifoon. restaurant.mu ⏱ 18.00–22.30 Mon, 12.00–23.30 Tues–Sun

**Happy Rajah £££** ❾ Classy Indian restaurant famous for jumbo prawns, tandoori, meat and vegetarian curries, delicately flavoured rice and traditional breads. ⓐ Royal Road, Grand Baie ❶ 263 2241 ⓦ www.happyrajah.com ⏱ 12.00–14.30, 18.00–20.30 daily ❶ Booking recommended

## AFTER DARK

### Pubs & clubs

**Banana Beach Club** Jazz, rock and blues fans won't be disappointed. Grab a table at the back for a quiet chat or sit beneath the huge banyan tree up front for ear-cracking sound. ⓐ Royal Road, beside the Caltex petrol station ⓣ 263 0326 ⓛ 10.00–02.00 Mon–Sat, 18.00–02.00 Sun

**Buddah Club** House music, two dance floors, friendly bar and vibrant ambience for energetic 20–30 somethings. Crowded at weekends. ⓐ Chemin Vingt-Pieds ⓣ 263 1769/465 4259 ⓦ www. buddahclub.com ⓔ buddahclub@beegoogroup.com ⓛ 22.00–05.00 Wed, Fri & Sat, closed Mon, Tues, Thur & Sun

**The Godfather ££** Sophisticated nightclub on two floors attracting mature night owls. Two dance floors and five bars, including a champagne bar, VIP alcoves and a Mediterranean-style restaurant. Pop, electro and house music, plus monthly theme nights. ⓐ La Cuvette Beach, next to the Conference Centre ⓣ 263 3000 ⓛ 11.00–15.00, 19.00–24.00 Tues–Sat (restaurant), 22.30–04.00 Wed, Fri, Sat & eve of public holidays (club), closed Sun & Mon ⓘ Smart dress code

**Les Enfants Terribles** Exclusive and trendy nightclub. Dance, drink or chat – inside or out. ⓐ Royal Road, Pointe aux Canonniers ⓣ 263 8117 ⓔ lesenfants_terribles@intnet.mu ⓛ 22.00–06.00 Tues, Fri, Sat & eve of public holidays, closed Mon, Wed, Thur & Sun

**N-Gyone** Subdued lighting, intimate alcoves and the latest sounds appealing to Grand Baie's cool young things. ⓐ Royal Road, Grand Baie ⓣ 263 7664 ⓛ 19.00–until last customer leaves, Tues–Sun, closed Mon

▲ The distinctive flamboyant tree, also known as a flame tree

# Pereybère

Just 3 km (1¼ miles) north from busy Grand Baie is the laid-back resort of Pereybère. Smaller and quieter than Grand Baie, its main attraction is the pretty public beach. Modest accommodation, internet cafés, bars, shops and restaurants are all within easy walking distance, making it popular with independent holidaymakers. The resort is well served by buses, and plenty of tour operators are on hand to organise excursions and car hire.

⬤ A glass-bottom boat is the perfect way to see Mauritius' marine life

Safety buoys restrict the main swimming area and the coast is indented with rocky coves from where you can watch gorgeous sunsets. You can hire a sunbed, or take to the water and windsurf, snorkel or mess around in a pedalo or a glass-bottom boat. At weekends, fruit sellers expertly prepare pineapples and chop coconuts in the large tree-shaded car park behind the beach, competing with fast-food stalls selling hot fried rice and noodles.

## THINGS TO SEE & DO

### Galerie du Moulin Cassé
Local artist Diane Henry showcases her work and that of other artists in this tastefully renovated sugar mill, built in 1820. Embedded in the vaulted ceilings are 20,000 terracotta pots, making the building a unique architectural wonder.
ⓐ Old Mill Road ⓣ 727 0672/263 0672 ⓔ moulincasse@intnet.mu
ⓛ 10.00–18.00 Fri or by appointment

### Watersports
For parasailing, diving, big-game fishing, waterskiing, banana boat and speedboat trips, plus a variety of excursions across the length and breadth of the island, contact **Top Travel & Tours**.
ⓐ Royal Road ⓣ 263 4225 ⓔ toptravelandtours@yahoo.com

## TAKING A BREAK

**Cafeteria Pereybère £** Casual beach restaurant dishing up Chinese, Creole and European food. One of the few places where you can stroll off the beach in your swimwear and nobody bats an eyelid. ⓐ Pereybère Beach ⓣ 263 8539 ⓛ 10.00–21.30 daily

**Sealovers ££** Contemporary décor attracts a young crowd to this romantic seafood restaurant ⓐ Pereybère Beach ⓣ 263 6299 ⓦ www.sealovers.mu ⓛ 11.00–24.00 daily

# Grand Gaube

Grand Gaube, a small, friendly fishing village, sits on the remote northeastern tip of Mauritius. It's a quiet hideaway, perfect for a relaxing beach holiday. With only two hotels, Legends, and Paul and Virginie, Grand Gaube has retained much of its native charm. If you're on an all-inclusive package it's worth stepping outside your hotel and exploring the village and the surrounding area for a glimpse of simple local life.

## BEACHES

The public beach flanking Paul and Virginie Hotel is nicely landscaped and equipped with toilets, a children's play area and seating. Eating options are limited, but there are a couple of snack stalls along the beach. Local fishermen may offer to take you to Pointe Bernache for the day or you could jump on a bus for a ride north through sugar-cane-covered countryside to the idyllic beach of Anse la Raie.

## THINGS TO SEE & DO

### Goodlands

To experience the bustle of a densely populated Mauritian town, head inland to Goodlands. Browse the shops and visit the market (open Tuesdays and Fridays), famous for textiles and clothing at knock-down prices. You can also watch craftsmen opposite at **Historic Marine**, the island's biggest model ship builders.

🅐 Goodlands, 4.8 km (3 miles) southwest of Grand Gaube 🅣 283 9404 🅦 www.historic-marine.com 🅛 08.00–17.00 Mon–Fri, 09.00–12.00 Sat & Sun

### Pointe Bernache

This little-visited uninhabited island to the southeast of Grand Gaube makes a wonderful day out for swimming, snorkelling and walking. Take something to eat and drink and a sun hat. Ask your hotel rep for details.

# Belle Mare

Long white beaches, championship golf courses and some of the
island's finest hotels draw visitors to the rural isolation of Belle Mare.
Fanned all year round by the southeast trade winds, the resort draws in
sea lovers, golfers, honeymooners and families seeking peace and quiet.
The dreamy coast road winds from the rock-studded shores of Roches
Noires north of Belle Mare to Palmar and the indented coves of Trou
d'Eau Douce to the south.

Beautiful Belle Mare beach is hugely popular at the weekend. Behind
the beach locals quietly tend small vegetable plots and others have
opened souvenir shops in the simple village nearby. For chaotic island life
head to Centre de Flacq for its daily fruit and vegetable market, fast-food
snack stalls and jumble of shops.

## THINGS TO SEE & DO

### Waterpark
A fun activity for the whole family! Rides include giant slides, the
Mushroom Shower and something called The Black Hole.
ⓐ Belle Mare ⓣ 415 2626 ⓛ 10.00–16.00 daily (summer), 10.00–15.30
daily (winter) ⓘ Admission charge; children under three free

## TAKING A BREAK

**Symon's ££** For a change from hotel dining there's an extensive menu
of Creole, Chinese and European food in this pleasant, casual restaurant.
ⓐ Belle Mare ⓣ 415 1135 ⓛ 10.00–22.00 daily

**La Maison d'Été £££** Go for the beef fillet or fish steak wrapped in a
banana leaf at this stylish family-run restaurant. ⓐ Poste Lafayette
ⓣ 410 5039 ⓦ www.lamaisondete.com ⓔ info@lamaisondete.com
ⓛ 18.00–22.00 Mon, 12.00–14.30, 18.00–22.00 Tues–Sat, closed Mon
lunch & Sun

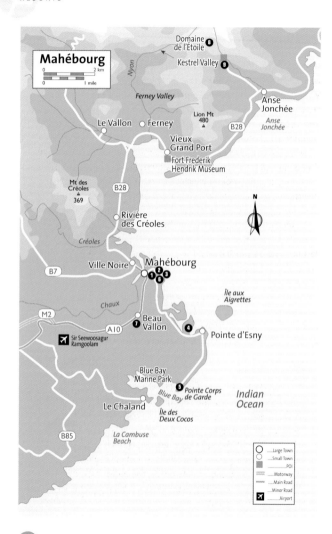

Mahébourg

# Mahébourg

Mahébourg (pronounced *May-burg*), a bustling town in the southeast, was named after Mahé de La Bourdonnais, the first French governor of Mauritius. Nestling on the southern shore of Vieux Grand Port, the scene of Mauritius' greatest naval battle between the French and British (see below), the town and the area around it are crammed with historic landmarks and eco-tourism attractions.

Mahébourg is ramshackle in places but a stroll through its narrow streets, named after early European settlers, brings you to the central market (open daily) around which tumbledown shops and cheap and cheerful eateries contrast with a modern supermarket and breezy waterfront overlooking the islet of Mouchoir Rouge.

Grand hotels such as Shandrani, beside a glistening lagoon, and Le Preskil, with views of Lion Mountain and the nature island of Île aux Aigrettes, provide everything for a beach holiday. And if you've made the long flight from Europe, the upside is that these hotels are only a 10-minute transfer from the airport.

Gentle hills swathed in sugar cane to the north of Mahébourg appear to tumble into the reef-fringed lagoon. This is the place to explore the verdant landscapes of Kestrel Valley, go hiking in the Ferney Valley, discover Dutch ruins or head south to Blue Bay, a designated marine

## THE BATTLE OF GRAND PORT

Under the French, Mauritius was known as *Île de France*. Many pirates and corsairs made it a base from which to attack ships belonging to British East India Company. In 1810 the attacks reached such alarming proportions that the British launched a huge, but unsuccessful naval attack in Mahébourg bay, where many gunships foundered on reefs. A few months later they landed on the north coast, captured the island from the French and renamed it Mauritius.

park, where you can hire watersports equipment or enjoy glass-bottom boat rides and fun cruises.

## BEACHES

Most townsfolk use Mahébourg's renovated waterfront as a pleasant area to sit and watch fishermen bringing in their catch from pretty pirogues, rather than to swim. The grassy areas are dotted with statues of Indian gods and temples, a few mobile snack stalls and an obelisk commemorating the Battle of Grand Port.

### Blue Bay

Apart from the beaches surrounding Le Preskil Hotel to the south of town, the best public beach is at Blue Bay, just beyond the residential area of Pointe d'Esny.

⬤ *Île des Deux Cocos sits off the coast at Blue Bay*

Blue Bay certainly lives up to its name. The gorgeous azure lagoon is backed by a crescent of soft shelving sand shaded by casuarina trees. Like many public beaches in Mauritius it's pretty chaotic at weekends with picnicking families, but midweek it makes a quiet getaway. On the south side of the bay is the sand-belted **Île des Deux Cocos**, once a holiday retreat for the late Princess Margaret and nowadays a romantic place to tie the knot. Local entrepreneurs, who will usually spot you before you spot them, often include Île des Deux Cocos on their tours of the lagoon.

Blue Bay is an equally wonderful place for windsurfing, and there are some great diving spots nearby, including shipwrecks within the lagoon at Vieux Grand Port.

## La Cambuse

Situated 3.5 km (2 miles) south of the airport is the deserted public beach of La Cambuse, at the end of a rough track on the right just before reaching the entrance to the Shandrani Hotel. It's a long, wild, natural beach blessed with white sands shelving sharply into a deep lagoon. There are strong currents here so take note of the warning signs. Bring a towel and something to lie on and maybe enjoy a picnic.

## THINGS TO SEE & DO

### Blue Bay Marine Park

This marine park is a hit with water lovers for its diverse and plentiful marine life and coral gardens. The visitor centre (closed for renovation until 2012), manned by fisheries protection officers 24 hours a day, provides advice on marine conservation and information on fish species to look out for, including those you'll find on a menu, such as the *licorne* (unicorn) fish and *vieille rouge* (grouper). The park is divided into several zones, each indicated by coloured buoys, for swimming, snorkelling, glass-bottom boating, waterskiing and mooring of boats.

**Blue Bay Marine Park visitor centre** ⓐ Blue Bay ⓣ 631 3940

> ## DOING YOUR BIT FOR MARINE CONSERVATION
> - Don't stand or walk on corals.
> - Don't touch or feed any fish or marine life.
> - Don't collect shells or corals from the park.
> - Don't drop litter.

### Ferney Valley & Domaine de l'Étoile

Discover endemic flora and fauna in Ferney Valley. The visitor centre highlights conservation projects to save Mauritius' dwindling native forests. The streams and valleys of Domaine de l'Étoile to the north offer quad biking, cycling, trekking, archery and jeep safaris. Book through your hotel rep.

ⓐ Ferney Valley, north of Mahébourg ⓣ 433 1010 ⓦ www.cieletnature.com (French language only) ⓘ Admission charge; guided tours only

### Fort Frederik Hendrik Museum

Occupying the site of a 17th-century Dutch fort on which the French later built their own defences, this small museum contains artefacts dating back to the Dutch settlement along with a model of the original fort.

ⓐ Royal Road, Vieux Grand Port ⓣ 634 4319 ⓛ 09.00–16.00 Mon, Tues & Thur–Sat, closed Wed, Sun & public holidays

### Île aux Aigrettes

Giant tortoises, bands of pink pigeons and lively geckos live happily amid indigenous flora. The island, managed by the Mauritius Wildlife Foundation, successfully showcases what Mauritius was like before humans stepped ashore. Book through your hotel or direct on ⓣ 631 2396 ⓦ www.mauritian-wildlife.org ⓘ Admission charge; guided tours only

### Kestrel Valley

Trek through wooded pathways bounded by indigenous trees, watch the recently endangered Mauritius kestrel being hand-fed and

enjoy Creole cuisine in the hilltop restaurant with views of Grand Port.

ⓐ Anse Jonchée ① 634 5011/5097 ⓦ www.kestrelvalley.com

① 08.30–16.30 daily

### Mahébourg Market

This bustling market draws hundreds of people from all over the island for textiles, baskets, spices and knick-knacks at low prices.

ⓐ Near the bus station ① 08.00–16.00 Mon

### Mahébourg National History Museum

History buffs can browse at the exhibits in this 300-year-old colonial mansion, which saw time as a hospital during the Franco–British naval conflict.

ⓐ Royal Road, Mahébourg ① 631 9329 ① 09.00–16.00 Mon & Wed–Fri, 09.00–12.00 Sat, Sun & public holidays, closed Tues

## TAKING A BREAK

**Dragon de Chine £** ❶  Bright yellow tables on a terrace fringed by potted plants and flowers lend a cheerful atmosphere to this small, simple restaurant specialising in seafood and Chinese and Creole cuisine. ⓐ Rue Flamand, Mahébourg ① 631 0698 ① 631 0697

① 10.30–23.30 daily

**Monte Carlo £** ❷  For straightforward Creole and Chinese food this centrally located restaurant comes up trumps. Don't be put off by its uninspiring location overlooking the bus station. ⓐ Rue de la Passe, Mahébourg ① 631 7449 ① 09.00–16.00, 18.00–22.00 Wed–Mon, closed Tues

**P'tit Coeur Waterfront Café £** ❸  Simple takeaways include *gateau patate* (sweet potato cake) and *gateau du pain* (fried savoury bread). Sit-down meals at the adjacent café. ⓐ Traffic Centre, Mahébourg

① 291 0582/731 2993 ① 08.00–18.00 daily

**La Belle Kréole ££ ❹**   Enjoy the free pre-dinner pirogue trip before tucking into authentic Creole cuisine at this waterside restaurant. Try the local stew or *rougaille* (a sauce made from tomatoes, onion,

⬤ *Monument commemorating the battle of Grand Port, Mahébourg*

garlic and ginger) and home-made coconut ice cream. ⓐ Coast Road, Pointe d'Esny ❶ 631 5037 Ⓦ www.leclubdesgrandsbois.com/labellekreole ❶ 10.00–15.00, 18.00–22.30 daily
❶ Reservations recommended

**Le Bougainville ££** ❾ Casual beach-facing eatery with picnic tables, packed at weekends, serves pasta, pizza and a good selection of Creole food. ⓐ Pointe d'Esny road, Blue Bay ❶ 631 8299 ❶ 10.00–22.00 daily

**Les Copains d'Abord ££** ❻ Nautical-themed eatery on the waterfront offers Creole cuisine, game and seafood. Friendly staff, catering to a largely young crowd and with a lively ambience. ⓐ Rue Sivananda, Mahébourg ❶ 631 9728 ⓔ lescopains@intnet.mu ❶ 10.00–15.00, 18.00–22.30 daily

**Le Jardin de Beau Vallon ££** ❼ This restored colonial house is surrounded by gardens and is noted for its fusion of Mauritian and European cuisine. Bungalow accommodation available on site. ⓐ Beau Vallon ❶ 631 2850 Ⓦ www.beau-vallon.net ❶ 11.00–15.00, 18.30–22.00 daily ❶ Reservations recommended

**L'Étoile £££** ❽ Enjoy the typically Mauritian venison curry and other traditional fare at this stylish thatch-roofed riverside restaurant. It is a popular stop-off for exploring the Ferney Valley nearby. ⓐ Domaine de l'Étoile, southeast of Montagne Blanche ❶ 433 1010 Ⓦ www.cieletnature.com (French language only) ❶ 11.00–14.00 daily ❶ Reservations only

**Le Kestrel Restaurant £££** ❾ Relax in this hilltop restaurant giving panoramic views of the bay where the Battle of Grand Port took place in 1810. Go for the house speciality, venison curry. ⓐ Anse Jonchée ❶ 634 5011/5097 ❶ 634 5261 ❶ 11.00–16.00 daily ❶ Reservations recommended

# Bel Ombre

Bel Ombre lies at the western end of Mauritius' long, wild, remote south coast where an 18-hole championship golf course (see page 103) attracts lovers of the sport. Wining and dining, kids' clubs, free watersports and a range of land-based activities are provided by a line-up of sophisticated hotels catering to families and couples.

Spacious pool areas compensate for the narrow beaches, and hotel bars and restaurants provide ample entertainment. Even if you're on an all-inclusive deal it's worth leaving your hotel to explore a delectably rugged coastline, interspersed with the white beaches of **Pointe aux Roches** and **Pomponette**, which meander east to **Gris-Gris**, near Souillac.

## THINGS TO SEE & DO

### Robert Edward Hart Memorial Museum (La Nef)
The coral-built former bungalow of Mauritius' famous writer and poet has breathtaking views of the sea-battered cliffs at Gris-Gris.
ⓐ Souillac ⓣ 625 6101 ⓛ 09.00–16.00 Mon & Wed–Fri, 09.00–12.00 Sat, closed Tues, Sun & public holidays

### Valriche Forest
This 1,400-hectare (3,500-acre) private forest is perfect for nature walks, but if you want to step up a gear there are also quad-biking and 4WD excursions.
ⓐ Bel Ombre ⓣ 623 5615 ⓦ www.domainedebelombre.mu
ⓔ frederica@domainedebelombre.mu

### La Vanille Réserve des Mascareignes
This nature reserve contains 1,500 Nile crocodiles in safe enclosures, giant Aldabra tortoises, deer, bats and wild boar, an insectarium and a jungle adventure playground. The shop sells goods made from the skin of farmed crocodiles and you can tuck into croc-meat snacks in the cafeteria.
ⓐ Rivière des Anguilles ⓣ 626 2503 ⓦ www.lavanille-reserve.com ⓛ 09.30–17.00 daily ⓘ Admission charge; guided tours; insect repellent essential

# Le Morne

Le Morne is a verdant beach-belted peninsula in the southwest corner of Mauritius, crowned by the looming 555-m (1,820-ft) granite and basalt rock known as Le Morne Brabant.

There are no shops or restaurants nearby, but the gorgeous lagoons attract sun-worshippers and water-lovers to four fabulous hotels spread along pristine beaches. Golfers are drawn to the undulating 18-hole course at Le Paradis Hotel (see page 103) and there are plenty of hotel-based activities for children. If you want to get out and about, you will have to hire a car or taxi.

● *Looking towards Le Morne from the Black River district*

**A SYMBOL OF SLAVERY**

During the 18th and early 19th centuries, runaway slaves hid from their masters in the wooded slopes and caves of Le Morne Brabant. Now on the UNESCO World Heritage List, the mountain has become a symbol of the slaves' fight for freedom. Legend has it that one day the runaway slaves flung themselves off the mountain and into the sea when they saw an expedition travelling up the mountain. They preferred to die rather than allow themselves to be recaptured. Had they stayed in hiding they would have found out that the expedition, far from coming to apprehend them, had come to tell them that they were free. Slavery was abolished on Mauritius in 1835 and is now commemorated annually by a national holiday on 1 February.

## THINGS TO SEE & DO

### Helicopter tour

Don't fancy riding the waves? Then book the sightseeing trip of a lifetime hovering over the picture-postcard lagoons, spectacular mountains and pristine beaches of the southwest coast. Go for a 15-minute flip or the whole hog for an hour. Contact your rep or **Air Mauritius Helicopters** (❶ 603 3754 ❶ 637 4104 Ⓦ www.airmauritius. com/helicopter.htm ❷ helicopter@airmauritius.com).

### Kite-surfing

This sport is a big hit at Le Morne with strong winds testing even the most adept athlete. Indian Resort Hotel, near the famous 'One Eye' wave sought by surfers, is renowned for its facilities at Club Mistral International, where beginners can learn to glide the waves using top-notch equipment. Comprehensive three-day windsurfing and bodysurfing courses are on offer too. Book through **Indian Resort Hotel** (❶ 401 4200) or contact your rep.

## Watersports & trekking

As a hotel guest, free watersports, such as windsurfing, snorkelling, canoeing, pedalo and glass-bottom boat rides, are part of the package, with additional charges for diving and big-game fishing. For trekking, contact Yan at ⓣ 785 6177 ⓦ www.trekkingilemaurice.com

## TAKING A BREAK

**Face à la Mer £** Pretty guesthouse with shady veranda serves authentic Creole cuisine in the heart of a fishing village overlooking Îlot Fourneau. ⓐ 41 L'Embrasure Village ⓣ 252 8393 ⓦ www.facealamer.mu ⓔ facealamer@intnet.mu ⓛ 12.00–16.00 Mon–Sat, closed Sun ⓘ Dinner on reservation

**West Coast Pizza ££** This popular pizza restaurant is in the heart of the nearby village, La Gaulette, and draws locals and tourists from far and wide. The delicious pizzas are excellent value and come in varying sizes to suit your appetite. ⓐ Route Royale, La Gaulette ⓣ 451 5910 ⓛ 10.00–20.00 Wed–Mon, closed Tues

**Chateau de Bel Ombre £££** Fine dining in a colonial château overlooking a golf course. ⓐ Domaine de Bel Ombre ⓣ 623 5522 ⓦ www.domaine debelombre.mu ⓔ info@domainedebelombre.com ⓛ 18.30–22.30 daily ⓘ Reservations recommended

**Sirokan £££** Relax on the dinky veranda of this log-cabin-style restaurant with a mid-morning coffee or a tasty baguette. Alternatively, go for a full Creole meal in the cosy ambience of the restaurant inside. ⓐ Route Royale, La Gaulette ⓣ 451 5115 ⓛ 09.00–15.00, 18.00–22.00 daily

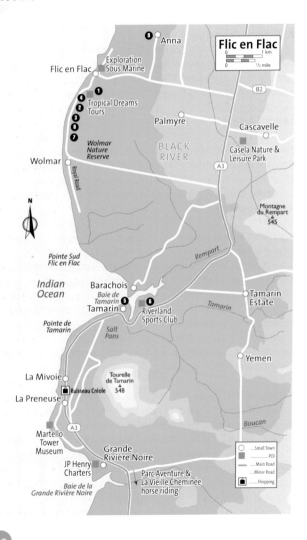

Flic en Flac

Anna

Exploration Sous Marine

Flic en Flac

**1** Tropical Dreams Tours

Palmyre

Cascavelle

Casela Nature & Leisure Park

Wolmar Nature Reserve

BLACK RIVER

Wolmar

Royal Road

Montagne du Rempart 545

Pointe Sud Flic en Flac

Rempart

Indian Ocean

Barachois

Baie de Tamarin

Tamarin Estate

Tamarin

Riverland Sports Club

Pointe de Tamarin

Salt Pans

Yemen

La Mivoie

Ruisseau Créole

Tourelle de Tamarin 548

La Preneuse

Boucan

Martello Tower Museum

A3

Grande Rivière Noire

JP Henry Charters

Parc Aventure & La Vieille Cheminée horse riding

Baie de la Grande Rivière Noire

Small Town
POI
Main Road
Minor Road
Shopping

# Flic en Flac

Flic en Flac, midway along the west coast, began as a low-key seaside spot used mainly by the townsfolk of Quatre Bornes and Rose Hill but in recent years has developed into a thriving international resort. It is set to rival Grand Baie (see page 15) with shops, cafés, bars and restaurants lining the coast road. Holiday apartments and small hotels at the busier north end and top-notch hotels at the quieter south end at **Wolmar** complement a beautiful 6-km (4-mile)-long sandy beach, which is backed by casuarina trees and has views of Le Morne Brabant in the distance.

Backed by rising sugar-cane fields, pocket-size mountain ranges and the numerous peaks of the Black River, there are lots of inland attractions around Flic en Flac to discover if you're looking to combine a beach holiday with both nightlife and nature. With its proximity to Port Louis and the plateau towns, there's some exciting shopping too.

Wolmar paints a picture of hedonism with luxury beach-resort hotels offering grand accommodation, watersports and lively nighttime entertainment. You can walk north along the lovely beach by day but if you want nightlife beyond your hotel you will need to hire a taxi or car to get to Flic en Flac.

Beyond Wolmar is the salt-making village and surfer's retreat of **Tamarin**, with a few small hotels lining a deep bay filled year round with playful dolphins. The River Tamarin flows into the bay and is backed by Rempart Mountain. Rising like a mini-Matterhorn, the views across the river are particularly romantic at sunset. For more active pursuits head to the modern Riverland Sports Club, which has a swimming pool, tennis courts and a cafeteria.

Further south, big-game fishermen are drawn to the area of **Black River** (Grande Rivière Noire), an up-and-coming district, thanks to the Ruisseau Créole shopping complex (ⓦ www.ruisseaucreole.com), noted for its designer shopping and smart restaurants. It's a hip place to see and be seen in and makes a handy stop if you're heading inland to Chamarel and the mysterious depths and misty mountains of **Black River**

◆ *Bougainvillea in bloom along Flic en Flac beach*

**Gorges National Park** (see page 82). Tiny Black River village itself has some colourful stores and eateries, but also look out for the old colonial-style post office and cemetery containing the grave of Colonel Draper (see page 68), and the **Martello Tower Museum** (see page 46).

## BEACHES

### Flic en Flac

Kick off your shoes and relax on this wide sandy beach where just about anything goes. The sands shelve gently into the lagoon so swimming is a delight. Do stick to the designated swimming areas and take notice of the 'dangerous bathing' signs at the north end as there are strong currents. Midweek, when it's not so busy, you can sit beneath the shade of fixed thatched umbrellas, hire a sunbed or picnic among the casuarina trees. There are toilets and parking areas, and plenty of mobile food wagons are on hand to dish up everything from chicken and chips to Creole specialities like spicy *poisson vindaye*, *faratha légume* and *poulet briani*. Alternatively, pop into any of the restaurants for a sit-down meal. At the far north end of the beach, in front of Villas Caroline Hotel, a sparkling sand spit welcomes sunbathers and snorkellers, but if you're after peace and quiet, head south.

### Tamarin

You can walk south along the beach from Wolmar or drive along the A3 to reach the natural, unspoilt public beach at Tamarin. The bay is popular with the surfing set and you can hire boards in the village.

### Wolmar

Stylish hotels, complete with sunbeds and watersports, dominate the beach at Wolmar. As a non-guest you'll be denied entry via the hotel entrance. The only way of accessing the boathouses is via the public beach, which is sandwiched between the Hilton and Sugar Beach Hotels and backed by the shade of casuarina trees. There are public toilets, a parking area and a few mobile snack stalls.

**RESPONSIBLE DIVING**

In the 1980s, to counter damage to the reef and the depletion of marine life at Flic en Flac, the Mauritius Marine Conservation Society deliberately sunk two tugs off the coast to create an artificial reef, which is now home to giant moray eels and colourful reef fish. Eco-friendly **Exploration Sous Marine** remains deeply involved in the project, and will take experienced divers to explore these sites.

ⓐ c/o Villas Caroline, Flic en Flac ⓣ 453 8450
ⓦ www.pierre-szalay.com ⓔ szalay@intnet.mu

## THINGS TO SEE & DO

### Big-game fishing

This year-round activity brings in tuna, bonito, wahoo and sailfish with October to April being the best months to hook blue and black marlin. Fully equipped boats leave from Black River.
Contact **JP Henry Charters** ⓐ Black River ⓣ 483 5038/729 0901
ⓦ www.blackriver-mauritius.com ⓔ info@blackriver.com

### Casela Nature and Leisure Park

The west coast's top attraction makes an action-packed day out. Go quad-biking, trekking, join a safari photo excursion and see zebras and antelope, walk in the wild with lions and cheetahs, visit the zoo and look out for the pink pigeon and Mauritius kestrel among the hundreds of species of birds in the aviaries. For children, there's a petting area containing ostriches, deer, goats and tame parrots. Finish off in the hilltop cafeteria for stunning views of countryside and coast or pack a picnic to enjoy on the lawns.
ⓐ Cascavelle ⓣ 452 2828/727 6076 ⓕ 452 0694 ⓦ www.caselayemen.mu
ⓔ casela@intnet.mu ⓛ 09.00–17.00 daily, closed Christmas and New Year's Day ⓘ Admission charge; reservations recommended for some activities

## Dolphin-watching

Your hotel can arrange a catamaran cruise to Île aux Bénitiers, an uninhabited long, flat sandbank. The half-day trip leaves from Black River and includes a morning with dolphins followed by snorkelling and lunch. For a specific dolphin-watching trip contact **Tropical Dreams Tours** (ⓐ Octagon Tower, Coast Road, Flic en Flac ⓣ 453 8480/764 0329 ⓦ www.tropic-dream.com ⓔ tropicdream@intnet.mu).

## Horse riding

Horses can be hired by the hour for great beach and country rides. A recommended company is **La Vieille Cheminée** (ⓐ Chamarel ⓣ 483 5249/725 5546 ⓦ www.lavieillecheminee.com) ⓘ Booking essential

◐ Walk with lions at Casela Nature and Leisure Park

> ### BE DOLPHIN FRIENDLY
> Before booking a dolphin-watching trip make sure your operator is properly licensed. Never feed the dolphins and never chase or harass them, especially if they are with their young.

### Martello Tower Museum

Built by the British to repel invaders, this Martello tower, now operating as a museum, contains fine examples of a powder magazine, artillery store and original living quarters.

🅐 La Preneuse, Black River ❶ 471 0178 🕐 09.00–17.00 Tues–Sat, 09.00–13.00 Sun, closed Mon ❶ Admission charge

### Parc Aventure

Test your stamina on guided botanic excursions along treetop roped walkways of varying difficulties in the heart of a thick forest. Wear comfortable clothing and trainers and use insect repellent. Safety harnesses are provided. Lunch is available on site if you have worked up an appetite.

🅐 Chamarel ❶ 234 5385 🅦 www.parc-aventure-chamarel.com
🅔 parcaventure@intnet.mu 🕐 09.30–16.00 daily ❶ Admission charge; reservations essential

## TAKING A BREAK

**Black Steer ££** ❶ Reliable breakfasts, steaks, fish and chips, and grills are served in this popular hangout. 🅐 Pasadena Complex, Royal Road ❶ 453 8590 🅔 blacksteer@intnet.mu 🕐 07.30–23.00 daily

**Chez Pepe ££** ❷ Long-established Italian eatery with tables on a shaded terrace overlooking the beach. Worth leaving your hotel for the generous pizza and pasta portions or just for a drink. Try the fish *carpaccio* and finish with *grappa* or *sambuca*. 🅐 Royal Road ❶ 453 9383

barbera@intnet.mu 11.30–15.00, 18.30–22.00 Sun–Thur, 11.30–15.00, 18.30–23.00 Fri & Sat

**Haveli ££** ❸   This classy upstairs restaurant turns out Indian specialities, grills and tandoori. Oasis Complex, Royal Road /  453 5169 11.30–15.00, 18.00–23.00 daily

**Ocean ££** ❹   Tables are set around an ornamental pool in this spacious family restaurant with subtle splashes of Chinese décor. Try chicken or fish braised in a fresh ginger sauce, great seafood and hot *chatini*, washed down with jasmine tea. Royal Road 453 8549 453 8514 www.oceanrestaurant.com eat@oceanrestaurant.com 10.00–15.00, 18.00–22.00 daily

**La Terrasse ££** ❺   Jazz enthusiasts can enjoy themed buffet meals in this hotel-restaurant that overlooks well-tended gardens and a pool. Live

Flic en Flac's idyllic beach with Le Morne in the distance

music most nights in the adjacent bar.  Tamarin Hotel, Tamarin Bay
**1** 483 6927 **W** www.hoteltamarin.com **L** 19.00–22.00 daily

**Ze Melting Potes ££** ⬤   Trendy café-restaurant set in pleasant gardens
serving burgers, sandwiches and salads. ⓐ Riverland Sports Club
Barachois, Tamarin **1** 498 7400 **L** Mon–Thur 07.00–18.00, Fri 07.00–
21.00, Sun 07.00–15.00

**Zub Express ££** ⬤   International chefs turn out authentic Chinese,
Indian and Mauritian food and a good takeaway service is also available.
There's an Internet café and excursions can be arranged as well.
ⓐ 286 Royal Road **1** 453 8868 **W** http://zub-express.restaurant.mu
ⓔ zubrestaurant@orange.mu **L** 10.00–15.00, 18.00–22.00 Mon–Thur,
10.00–22.00 Sat & Sun, closed Fri

## AFTER DARK

**Shooters Bar ££** ⬤   Late-night haunt for steak and seafood with a
piano bar and live music at weekends. Try the chicken penne or if
you've been partying all night fill up on the cowboys' breakfast!
ⓐ Oasis Complex, Royal Road **1** 453 5607 **L** 08.00–23.00 Tues–Thur,
08.00–24.00 Fri–Sat, 08.00–18.00 Sun, closed Mon

**Twin's Gardens ££** ⬤   Tasty French and international cuisine at this
popular restaurant which has live music and dancing at weekends.
ⓐ Royal Road **1** 453 5250 ⓔ twinsgardens@hotmail.com **L** 12.00–15.00,
18.00–01.00 Tues–Sun, 18.00–01.00 Mon

**Domaine Anna £££** ⬤   Long-established Chinese restaurant set amid
waterfalls, ponds and gardens. Reserve a pavilion for privacy or eat in the
main restaurant. South African wines complement an extensive menu
that uses produce grown on the estate. ⓐ Medine **1** 453 9650
**W** www.domaineanna.net **L** 12.00–14.30, 17.30–22.30 Tues–Sun,
closed Mon

# Balaclava

Balaclava is a newcomer to the tourist scene in Mauritius and is showing all the signs of becoming an upmarket resort with an Integrated Resort Scheme (see box below) to complement six stylish hotels along its fine sandy beaches. Balaclava feels remote yet being only 9.5 km (6 miles) north of the capital, Port Louis, and within easy reach of Pointe aux Piments and Trou aux Biches, the area is a big draw for discerning beach lovers and also has attractions to call its own.

Service and accommodation score highly at the big-name hotels, like the Grand Mauritian and the Meridien, pioneers in operating an open-door policy to non-guests, with fabulous restaurants and buzzing bars. Indeed, these digs are so comfortable that you might be tempted to stay put, but it's worth getting out and about to visit some of the north's top attractions.

## BEACHES

### Balaclava

Flanked by the Oberoi and Victoria Hotels and backed by an elevated grassy picnic area, Balaclava is the quietest of all the public beaches along this coast. You can park anywhere on the grass and stroll left to reach the beach fronting the Oberoi as far as the River Citron, which flows into Tombeau Bay. Beyond the river on the other side of the bay are the Maritim, Grand Mauritian and InterContinental hotels and distant views of Port Louis' mountains. The area was declared the Balaclava

### YOUR OWN PATCH IN PARADISE?

Mauritian law allows foreigners to buy luxury villas under the Integrated Resort Scheme (IRS) with foreign residency as part of the deal. At Balaclava, an IRS scheme is under construction on the banks of the River Tombeau where villas will overlook an 18-hole golf course.

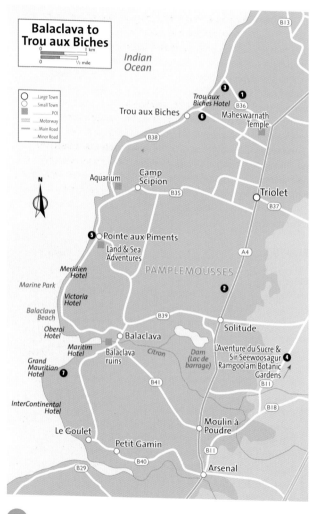

**Balaclava to
Trou aux Biches**

0 _____ 1 km
0 _____ 1/2 mile

Indian
Ocean

○ .....Large Town
○ .....Small Town
▪ .....POI
▭ .....Motorway
▭ .....Main Road
▭ .....Minor Road

N

Trou aux
Biches Hotel

Trou aux Biches

Maheswarnath
Temple

Triolet

Aquarium

Camp
Scipion

Pointe aux Piments
Land & Sea
Adventures

Meridien
Hotel

Marine Park

Victoria
Hotel

Balaclava
Beach

Oberoi
Hotel

Maritim
Hotel

Balaclava

Balaclava
ruins

Citron

Dam
(Lac de
barrage)

Solitude

L'Aventure du Sucre &
Sir Seewoosagur
Ramgoolam Botanic
Gardens

PAMPLEMOUSSES

Grand
Mauritian
Hotel

InterContinental
Hotel

Le Goulet

Petit Gamin

Moulin à
Poudre

Arsenal

Marine Park in 1997 on account of its concentration of live corals. While turtle sightings are less common these days, there are plenty of lagoon fish such as snapper, wrasse and emperor to keep snorkellers entertained.

## Pointe aux Piments

This public beach to the north of Balaclava fronts Pointe aux Piments village, where you'll find public toilets, seating, shaded kiosks and a parking area. The quieter north end of the beach is interspersed with grassy picnic areas and rock pools and while not the best beach for swimming, this is compensated for by the gorgeous sunsets and wild beauty. On Fridays at dusk don't miss the *sega* dancers and musicians who perform their erotic dance on the beach in front of the Victoria Hotel.

### SEGA

This sensual dance, imported by African and Malagasy slaves when the island was under French rule, was traditionally performed around a fire at the end of a day's work. The lyrics recounted the plight of their captivity to the sound of drums and stringed instruments. Nowadays modernised versions of the *sega* take place in hotels but at weekends you'll stumble across impromptu performances on public beaches. Do join in, if invited, to this foot shuffling, hip-wiggling dance but remember a traditional *sega* involves no bodily contact with your partner!

## Trou aux Biches

This sugar-soft white 4-km (2½-mile) beach starts at the Fish Landing Station and hugs the coastline all the way to Mon Choisy. Private beachside villas and apartments occupy the southern end, but the busiest and most beautiful stretch borders the spacious grounds of the Trou aux Biches Hotel. Here speedboats and waterskiers zoom across the lagoon and fruit sellers and beach hawkers ply their goods. The lagoon is ideal for swimming and snorkelling, and individual operators are happy to rent you a windsurf board, pedalo or glass-bottom boat. There is little shade so take a sun hat and water if you plan to go beachcombing.

## THINGS TO SEE & DO

### Aquarium
Freshwater ponds and a circuit of tanks contain a rich variety of reef and lagoon marine life, including turtles, sharks and moray eels. The fish are fed daily at 11.00. There's a pleasant snack bar and shop.
ⓐ Coast Road, Pointe aux Piments ⓣ 261 4561 ⓦ www.mauritius aquarium.com ⓛ 09.30–17.00 Mon–Sat, 10.00–15.00 Sun & public holidays ⓘ Admission charge

⬥ The ruins of the arsenal and powder mill at Balaclava

## L'Aventure du Sucre

Follow Mauritius' historical trail from early sugar plantations to the modern day in this former sugar factory, which ranks as the country's finest museum.

ⓐ Beau Plan, Pamplemousses ☎ 243 7900 ⓦ www.aventuredusucre.com
🕑 09.00–17.00 daily, closed 24–26 & 31 Dec, 1 & 2 Jan
❶ Admission charge

## Balaclava ruins

These ruins are believed to have formed part of an 18th-century arsenal and powder mill, which supplied ammunition and ships for French expeditions to India. Walk through landscaped gardens to the sound of waterfalls, birdsong and the babbling of the River Citron where you can see the remains of the old sea walls and a rum distillery.

ⓐ Inside Maritim Hotel grounds, Balaclava ❶ Seek permission from the security guards at the entrance

## Diving & watersports

Take to the water with **Land & Sea Adventures**, a reputable company specialising in diving, cruising, watersports and excursions, including a catamaran trip and barbecue lunch to Plate and Gabriel islands.

ⓐ Pointe aux Piments, next door to Villas Mon Plaisir Hotel ☎ 261 1724
ⓦ www.villasmonplaisir.com 🕑 08.00–17.00 Mon–Sat, closed Sun

## Maheswarnath Temple

Tucked behind Triolet, the longest village in Mauritius, is this large colourful temple built in 1857. The friendly caretaker will show you round and you may leave a donation in the box beneath the banyan tree. You're welcome to take pictures but do remove your shoes if you go inside.

ⓐ Mariamen Road, Triolet 🕑 06.00–18.00 daily

## Sir Seewoosagur Ramgoolam Botanic Gardens

Enjoy a stroll in these world-famous gardens (known locally as Pamplemousses Botanic Gardens) and look out for talipot palms, lotus ponds and the amazing *Victoria amazonica* water lily. There's a giant tortoise enclosure and the 19th-century British-built Château Mon Plaisir.

ⓐ Pamplemousses ☏ 243 9403 ⓦ www.gov.mu/portal/site/ssrbg
🕓 08.30–17.30 daily ⓘ Admission charge; children under five free

## TAKING A BREAK

**Florensuc Patisserie £** ❶  Sausage rolls or banana tart go down well here with *espresso* or cappuccino served in a secluded courtyard. Takeaway orders too. ⓐ Trou aux Biches Road ☏ 265 5349
🕓 09.00–16.00 Mon–Sat, closed Sun

🔺 *Giant water lilies at the botanic gardens*

**Foley's Restaurant £ ❷** Good value and popular with locals for its typical Mauritian cuisine. Try the *briani*, noodles or go for a traditional curry. ⓐ Mile 7, Triolet Road ❶ 261 4533 ⏰ 10.00–22.00 daily

**Souvenir Snack £ ❸** Popular with beachgoers and locals, this cheerful shaded café offers filling fried rice and noodles. ⓐ Royal Road, Trou aux Biches ❶ 291 1440 ⏰ 11.00–23.00 daily

**Le Fangourin ££ ❹** Relaxing lunch stop overlooking the lawned gardens of L'Aventure du Sucre museum. The menu features Creole and European cuisine and delicious desserts made with speciality sugars. ⓐ Beau Plan ❶ 243 7990 ⓦ www.aventuredusucre.com ⏰ 10.00–15.00 daily

**Villas Mon Plaisir ££ ❺** Hamburgers, pizza, baguettes, sandwiches, salads and chips feature on the menu of this light, airy hotel restaurant overlooking the beach. ⓐ Pointe aux Piments ❶ 261 7980 ⓦ www.villas monplaisir.com ⏰ 08.00–22.00 daily

## AFTER DARK

**La Casa Negra ££ ❻** Salsa, sangria and a great dance floor complement the fusion of Creole, Mexican and Spanish cuisine at this friendly, locally run restaurant. Live music at weekends. ⓐ Trou aux Biches Coast Road ❶ 499 0756/265 5426 ⓔ lacasanegra@myt.mu ⏰ 11.30–15.00, 18.30–01.00 daily

**Brezza £££ ❼** This trendy Italian restaurant with its tastefully modern décor is worth splashing out on. Kick off with a cocktail, admire the pool and finish with a drink and live music at the Bar 68. ⓐ Grand Mauritian Hotel, Balaclava ❶ 204 1400 ⓦ www.thegrandmauritian.com ⏰ 12.30–15.00, 19.00–23.30 daily ❶ Smart casual dress

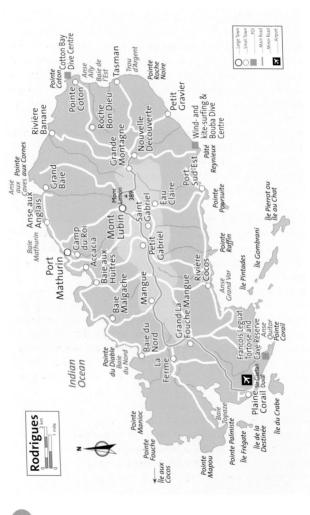

**Rodrigues**

Legend:
- Large Town
- Small Town
- POI
- Main Road
- Minor Road
- Airport

Indian Ocean

Pointe Coton — Cotton Bay, Cotton Bay Dive Centre
Anse Ally
Baie de l'Est
Tasman
Trou d'Argent
Pointe Coton
Pointe Roche Noire
Rivière Banane
Roche Bon Dieu
Petit Gravier
Anse aux Caves aux Cornes
Pointe aux Cornes
Grand Baie
Grande Montagne
Nouvelle Découverte
Wind- and kite-surfing & Bouba Dive Centre
Baie Mathurin
Anse aux Anglais
Mont Limon 389
Saint Gabriel
Sud-Est
Paté Reynieux
Camp du Roi
Mont Lubin
Eau Claire
Pointe Poursuite
Port Mathurin
Accacia
Petit Gabriel
Port Sud-Est
Île Pierrot ou Île du Chat
Baie aux Huîtres
Pointe Raffin
Île Gombrani
Baie Malgache
Mangue
Rivière Cocos
Anse Grand Var
Île Pintades
Grand La Fouche Mangue
Baie du Nord
François Leguat Tortoise and Cave Reserve
Anse Quitor Pointe Corail
Pointe du Diable
Baie du Nord
La Ferme
St-Gaetan
Île du Crabe
Plaine Corail
Anse Corail Duval
Pointe Manioc
Baie Topaze
Pointe Fouche
Île Frégate
Île de la Destinée
Pointe Palmiste
Pointe Mapou
Île aux Cocos

N

0 — 2 km
0 — 1 mile

# Rodrigues

The fish-shaped island of Rodrigues that lies east of Mauritius has long been a favourite with Mauritians seeking an escape from the stress of daily life. Until 2000 a handful of adventurous tourists would make the 36-hour sea voyage from Mauritius, but nowadays most visitors take the 90-minute flight, landing at the Sir Gaetan Duval Airport at Plaine Corail in the south. Some visitors stay for a week or so, to discover the authentic, sometimes quirky tropical island lifestyle that is so different from that of its more glamorous sister island, Mauritius.

Lying 560 km (348 miles) east of Mauritius, Rodrigues measures 18 km (11 miles) long and 8 km (5 miles) wide and is surrounded by a lagoon, twice its size and dotted with 18 islets. The rugged landscape is more reminiscent of the highlands of Scotland than a tropical island and the people are more Afro-Creole than on multicultural Mauritius. With only four hotels and a dozen friendly guesthouses, Rodrigues appeals to the get-away-from-it-all eco-conscious visitor, including Prince William, who spent part of his gap year studying the reefs and lagoons there.

Ongoing conservation efforts to restore Rodrigues to its original native habitat, such as reforestation programmes and the clearing of invasive plants, have met with success. More recently, a reintroduced colony of giant Aldabra tortoises shows all the signs of becoming a major eco-tourism attraction. The pristine reefs and lagoon, too, have a special appeal for divers and there are dozens of sites to explore. You can trek up steep hillsides, just like the locals, stopping at watering holes in

**GETTING THERE**
Air Mauritius flies regularly to Rodrigues but seats fill fast. Tour operators in Mauritius can arrange your trip or you can book from home through a specialist tour operator such as Sportif International (📞 01273 844919 🌐 www.sportif.travel).

tiny villages, stroll along beautiful beaches and coves in the east, go big-game fishing, or step ashore for a barbecue on deserted Île aux Cocos, noted for its colony of seabirds.

Most of Rodrigues' 40,000 inhabitants are farmers, fishermen or employed in tourism and live in small settlements and villages or in the capital, Port Mathurin. Yet for all its simplicity, this island has good roads, comfortable accommodation and authentic Creole food, especially in restaurants in Port Mathurin, where you'll also find the main bus station, banks and ATMs, small supermarkets and shops, a tourist office and helpful tour operators to arrange excursions.

## BEACHES

### Anse aux Anglais (English Bay)

Anse aux Anglais is a 15-minute stroll east from the capital, Port Mathurin. It overlooks a shallow lagoon, which at low tide exposes rocks and reefs where local women spear octopuses. Backed by grassy lawns and shaded casuarinas, it's a picturesque spot for relaxing. If you climb the steep road behind the beach to Pointe Venus Hotel and into the adjacent hills, there are panoramic views across the lagoon.

### Pointe Coton (Cotton Bay)

This beach, on the island's northeastern tip, has special appeal for sun-worshippers and divers who stay at the adjacent **Cotton Bay Hotel** (❶ 831 8001 Ⓦ www.cottonbayhotel.biz), where non-guests are also welcome to use the bar and restaurant. The wide, flat sands are framed by low coral cliffs and backed by a forest of casuarinas. Walking south you stumble across the deserted bays and coves of Anse Ally, St François and the evocatively named Trou d'Argent (Silver Hole) where you can swim or explore the protected forest at Tasman. There are no facilities on these beaches so take a sun hat, something to eat and drink and wear sturdy shoes. Alternatively, you can join a guided walk with **Rotourco** (ⓐ Rue François Leguat, Port Mathurin ❶ 831 0747 Ⓦ www.rotourco.com ⓔ rotourco@intnet.mu).

## Port Sud-Est

Getting to Port Sud-Est is arguably the most scenic drive in Rodrigues. You pass isolated villages and descend a series of gentle hairpin bends giving resplendent views across the lagoons of the south coast. Access to this wild wide beach is via steps from the **Mourouk Ebony Hotel**, which is perched on a steep cliff. The winds attract kite- and windsurfers. Enjoy a coastal walk to **Petit Gravier** to the east, passing shaded forests and stunning vistas of isolated beaches.

◔ *The road to Port Sud-Est*

**FRANÇOIS LEGUAT**

In 1691 the island's first settler was François Leguat, a Huguenot, who landed by accident with a band of adventurers fleeing religious persecution in Europe. He found the shores covered with turtles, tortoises and prolific birdlife and he lived on coconuts, fish and fresh water. After Leguat's return to Europe he wrote *Voyages and Adventures*, which even today makes fascinating reading for historians, naturalists and travellers.

## THINGS TO SEE & DO

### Diving

Top-name operators are:

**Cotton Bay Dive Centre** ✉ c/o Cotton Bay Hotel ☏ 831 8001
✉ diverod@intnet.mu ⏰ 09.00–16.00 daily, closed July–Aug
**Bouba Diving Centre** ✉ c/o Mourouk Ebony Hotel ☏ 832 3063
🌐 www.boubadiving.com ✉ boubadiving@intnet.mu
⏰ Closed June

### Fishing

Recommended fishing operators based at Port Mathurin include:
**Blue Water Fishing** ☏ 831 0919 🌐 www.bluewaterfishing-rodrigues.com
(French language only) ✉ bluewater@intnet.mu
**Rod Fishing Club** ☏ 875 0616 🌐 www.rodfishingclub.com
✉ contact@rodfishingclub.com
**BDPM Fishing** ☏ 831 2790 ✉ birgit.dirk@intnet.mu

### François Leguat Giant Tortoise and Cave Reserve

Allow at least half a day to visit this 20-hectare (50-acre) reserve showcasing thousands of Rodrigues' endemic plants and a colony of over 500 captive-bred giant Aldabra tortoises. Informative guides explain the origin and habitats of these gentle giants and you can safely explore

⬤ *Giant Aldabra tortoises are the stars of the show*

centuries-old limestone caves containing well-lit stalagmites and stalactites. A museum is devoted to the history and culture, and the flora and fauna of Rodrigues, there's an on-site cafeteria and you can even sponsor a tortoise!

ⓐ Plaine Caverne ⓣ 832 8141 ⓦ www.tortoisecavereserve-rodrigues.com
ⓛ 09.00–17.00 daily ❶ Admission charge; guided tours at 10.30, 12.30, 14.30

## Port Mathurin

Spend a morning in the colourful capital where the pace of life is definitely slow. It's easy to walk around and getting from one end of town to the other takes no more than half an hour. The best time is 06.00 on Saturday morning when a lively market takes place near the jetty. In Rue de la Solidarité you'll find places to eat, general shops and the tourist office, the latter housed inside the island's oldest building, a colonial house dating back to 1873. You can shop for baskets, straw hats and head-blowing Rodriguan chillies and lime pickles, which come packed in jars to take home.

## Windsurfing & kite-surfing

The best place for kite- and windsurfing is on the south coast. There are introductory courses for beginners, and the experienced can take advantage of special downwind trips.

**Osmosis Club** ⓐ c/o Morouk Ebony Hotel ⓣ 832 3051
ⓦ www.osmosis-rodrigues.com (French language only)
ⓔ osmosis@intnet.mu

> ### DEMISE OF THE RODRIGUES TORTOISE
> In 1761 an English fleet landed at Anse aux Anglais and for six months transported thousands of Rodrigues tortoises to Réunion and Mauritius, where they were highly prized for their meat. By the end of the 18th century the Rodrigues tortoise suffered the same fate as the Mauritian dodo and became extinct.

## TAKING A BREAK

**Bambous £** Cheerful décor and lovely sea views. Great stop for soft drinks and beer. The menu features seafood and pizza. ❸ Anse aux Anglais ❶ 832 0701 ❷ 10.00–22.00 daily

**Chue Wan Snack £** Snazzy snack bar with bright red chairs and picnic tables outside. Try *gateaux piments* (chilli cakes), *hakien* (bean-curd rolls), filled baguettes and chips. ❸ Rue de la Solidarité, Port Mathurin ❶ 831 1507 ❷ 09.00–15.00 Mon–Fri, closed Sat & Sun

**John Resto Pub £** Expect a traditional Rodriguan welcome at this rustic restaurant in the isolated hills, which offers octopus curry to die for. ❸ Mangue ❶ 831 6306 ❷ 11.00–15.00 Tues–Sun, closed Mon

**Le Nouveau Capitaine £** This long-established restaurant attracts locals and tourists for the excellent seafood, chicken dishes and a daily Rodriguan special. ❸ Johnston Street, Port Mathurin ❶ 831 1581 ❶ 831 1726 ❷ 10.00–15.00, 18.00–22.00 daily

**Paille en Queue £** Simple eatery for filling Chinese and Creole food. Tuck into stir-fried octopus or the local catch of the day. ❸ Rue François Leguat, Port Mathurin ❶ 832 0084 ❷ 10.00–22.00 daily

**Le Bois d'Olive ££** Spacious upmarket restaurant with individual dining areas offering panoramic views over Port Mathurin, first-class seafood and Rodriguan specials. Rooms for rent too. ❸ Mont Lubin Road, near Solitude ❶ 832 1071 ❷ 11.00–15.00, 18.00–22.00 daily

**Aux 2 Frères ££** First-floor restaurant with a smart shaded terrace, specialising in French and local fare. ❸ Rue François Leguat, Port Mathurin ❶ 831 0541 ❷ 11.00–15.00, 18.00–22.00 Tues–Sun, closed Mon

**La Détente ££** This hilltop family-run restaurant has the best views of the south coast lagoons. Try the *cono-cono* (see page 93) or octopus salads, seafood dishes, or settle for Chinese, European or Rodriguan fare. ❸ Eau Claire ❶ 832 5871 ❹ 11.00–15.00 daily ❶ Dinner on reservation

**Restaurant Chez Ram ££** Sophisticated by Rodriguan standards, this spacious colonial-style restaurant has views across the lagoon. It's a ten-minute walk east from Port Mathurin and is renowned for seafood, curries and super-hot chillies. ❸ Baie Lascares ❶ 832 0736 ❹ chezram@intnet.mu ❹ 08.30–14.30, 17.00–21.00 Thur–Tues, closed Wed

**Restaurant du Quai ££** Very popular lunch stop after visiting the Saturday market where you can dine on seafood, Indian, Mauritian and Rodriguan cuisine. ❸ Wolphart Harmensen Street, Port Mathurin ❶ 831 2840 ❹ chezram@intnet.mu ❹ 10.00–14.00, 18.00–21.00 Tues–Sun, closed Mon ❶ Booking advised

### CARING FOR THE DISABLED

Careco, a charitable organisation run by Englishman Paul Draper, includes a school for the hard of hearing and partially sighted, a workshop for the disabled, a gift shop and an apiary turning out honey that won a silver medal at London's National Honey Show. See how honey is made, and if you buy a pot to take home you'll be contributing to a very worthwhile cause.
❸ Camp du Roi ❶ 831 1766 ❹ 09.00–17.00 Mon–Fri, 09.00–12.00 Sat, closed Sun

❹ *The Black River Gorges*

 EXCURSIONS
Out & about

EXCURSIONS

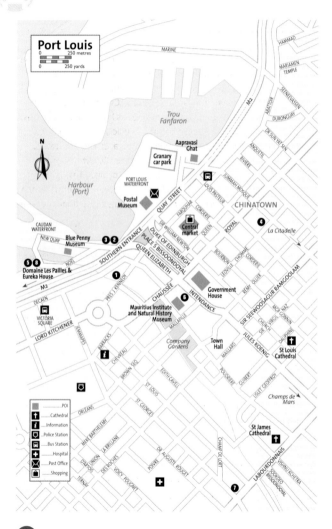

# Port Louis & around

In 1735 Mahé de Labourdonnais, the first French Governor-General of the Mascarene Islands, founded the capital, Port Louis. Sitting on the northwest coast, the city has a rich heritage, thanks to French and British colonists and immigrants from India, Africa and China who came and settled over the years. The city, named after Louis XV of France, is divided into two areas: Old Port Louis (the business district) and the modern Caudan Waterfront with shopping malls, restaurants and two hotels.

The Moka Mountains form a cradle round the city out of which a jumble of colonial buildings emerges, dwarfed by new soaring contemporary architecture. Allow half a day, preferably in the cool of the morning, to experience the chaotic vibrancy of this city and take in some history and culture.

## THINGS TO SEE & DO

### Aapravasi Ghat

In the 19th century half a million indentured Indian labourers landed at this depot, now a UNESCO World Heritage Site, to work in sugar plantations in conditions not far short of slavery. It's a symbolic site for Indo-Mauritians, who form three-quarters of the country's population.
ⓐ Port Louis Waterfront ⓣ 217 3156 ⓦ www.aapravasighat.org
ⓞ 09.00–16.00 Mon–Fri, closed Sat & Sun

### Blue Penny Museum

This restored colonial building exhibits stamps, artwork, old maps, coins and photographs depicting the history of Mauritius.

> **PARKING**
> Parking in town is a nightmare! Leave your car at The Granary car park or on the waterfront and walk. Wear sturdy shoes and watch out for poor pavements and deep gulleys!

ⓐ Caudan Waterfront ⓣ 210 8176 ⓕ 210 9243 ⓛ 10.00–17.00 Mon–Sat, closed Sun ⓘ Admission charge

## Central market

Tropical produce contrasts with herbs and spices, dried fish, baskets, bags and souvenirs in this bustling market. Shop, chat or barter just like the locals, with dozens of pavement sellers and hawkers in the crowded streets nearby.

ⓐ Queen Street ⓛ 06.00–16.00 Mon–Sat, 06.00–12.00 Sun

## Champs de Mars

Champs de Mars used to be a training ground for French soldiers billeted in the capital. Today it's the Mauritius Turf Club, the oldest in the southern hemisphere. Founded in 1812 by a British army officer, Colonel Edward Draper, horse racing draws huge crowds from May to September. The best views are from the Citadelle, built as a look-out post by the British.

ⓐ East of town at the end of Pope Hennessy Street

## Chinatown

A stroll through Chinatown's backstreets reflects the business and mystery of the Orient. You'll find everything under the sun, from ointments and medicines to firecrackers and barbecued food, along with shops, restaurants and colourful pagodas.

ⓐ The entrance is along Royal Street via a pagoda-like archway

## Domaine Les Pailles

This verdant retreat offers quad-biking, horse-drawn carriage and train rides, a mask museum, a spice garden, a replica of an old-time sugar mill, a rum distillery, several restaurants and a casino.
The Swami Vivekananda Conference Centre nearby is a fine example of futuristic architecture.

ⓐ South along the motorway at Pailles ⓣ 286 4225 ⓦ www.domaine lespailles.net ⓛ 10.00–17.30 daily ⓘ Admission charge

⬣ *Statue commemorating the capital's founder, Mahé de La Bourdonnais*

## Eureka House

Built in 1856, this architectural wonder, now a museum, is the ancestral home of the Franco-Mauritian Leclezio family. The owner takes you on a guided tour of the house, which has 109 doors, indigenous timber floors and high-ceilinged rooms replete with antiques. Take tea on the terrace, stroll in the grounds or book lunch.

ⓐ South along the motorway at Moka ❶ 433 2584 ❿ www.maison eureka.com ❷ 09.00–17.00 Mon–Sat, 09.00–15.30 Sun & public holidays ❶ Admission charge

◓ *Dodo souvenirs are easy to come by*

## Government House

This impressive colonial building at the top of Place d'Armes is the seat of government. The interior is not open to the public but you can look through the gates into the courtyard where there is a marble statue of Queen Victoria.

## Mauritius Institute and Natural History Museum

See a stuffed dodo among sharks, shell collections and displays of Mascarene birds in this 19th-century colonial building. The adjacent Company Gardens stand on a site once occupied by the French East India Company headquarters and make a welcome respite from the city heat.

ⓐ La Chaussée ❶ 210 1272 ❶ 09.00–16.00 Mon &Tues, Thur & Fri, 09.00–12.00 Sat, closed Wed, Sun and public holidays

## Postal Museum

Browse the precious stamps, 18th-century newspapers and anything to do with philately in the former General Post Office building constructed by the British in 1868.

ⓐ Quay Street, Port Louis Waterfront ❶ 213 4812 ⓦ www.mauritius post.mu ❶ 09.30–16.30 Mon–Fri, 09.30–15.30 Sat & public holidays, closed Sun ❶ Admission charge

## TAKING A BREAK

**Life Bar £** ❶ The décor of this trendy café reflects the minimalism of a modern airport lounge. Good for people-watching from the shaded terrace over tasty baguettes, sandwiches and salads. ⓐ President John Kennedy Street ❶ 212 6565 ❶ 08.30–17.30 Mon–Fri, closed Sat & Sun

**Mystic Masala £** ❷ Alfresco fast-food eatery with bright tables and umbrellas serving spicy Indian fare. Try the curries and tasty flatbreads (*faratha*) if you're hungry, and the *kulfi* ice cream (see page 94) to cool off. ⓐ Caudan Waterfront ❶ 210 2442 ❶ 10.30–21.30 daily

⬥ *Palm trees aplenty near Government House*

**Black Steer ££** ❸ Great harbour views from this first-floor restaurant, which feels like you're on the deck of a cruise ship. Grab a table on the terrace or enjoy the air conditioning inside. Succulent steaks, ribs and fish and chips, modern background music and friendly staff. ❸ Caudan Waterfront ❶ 211 9147 ❷ blacksteer@intnet.mu ❸ 11.30–23.30 daily

**City Orient ££** ❹ First-floor air-conditioned Chinese restaurant popular with locals serving excellent fixed-price all-you-can-eat lunch buffet in the heart of Chinatown. ❷ 34 Leoville L'Homme Street ❶ 213 6868 ❸ 11.30–14.00 Mon–Fri ❶ Reservations only on Sat & Sun

**Dolce Vita ££** ❺ Surrounded by hills, this is a refreshing change from the heat and bustle of Port Louis. Wooden tables beneath a shaded terrace overlook an inviting pool at this smart-casual restaurant

specialising in pizzas, pastas and salads. Don't forget your swimsuit!
🅐 Domaine Les Pailles 🕿 286 4225 🅦 www.domainelespailles.net
🕘 12.00–15.00, 19.00–23.00 Mon–Sat, 11.00–16.00 Sun

**La Flore Mauricienne ££** ❻ Port Louis' oldest restaurant dating back to the 19th century attracts city folk and tourists to its cosy air-conditioned dining area and shaded pavement terrace. Daily Creole specials, patisserie, drinks and takeaway service. 🅐 10 Intendance Street
🕿 212 2200 📧 laflore@intnet.mu 🕘 08.30–17.00 Mon–Fri, 08.30–13.00 Sat, closed Sun

**Le Jardin ££** ❼ Authentic Creole dishes along with daily specials are served up in a romantic garden setting away from the noise of the town.
🅐 27 Rue St Georges 🕿 211 9688 📧 dchasseur@intnet.mu 🕘 10.00–16.30 Mon–Fri, closed Sat & Sun ❶ Dinner by reservation only; free car park

🔺 *The Caudan Waterfront in Port Louis*

**Indra £££** ❽ Classy Indian food is served by waiters in traditional costume at this restaurant noted for its décor of silk curtains and antique furniture from Rajasthan. ❷ Domaine Les Pailles ❶ 286 4225 Ⓦ www.domainelespailles.net ❶ 12.00–14.00, 19.00–22.30 Mon–Sat, closed Sun & public holidays ❶ Reservations advised

⬥ Outside the central market in Port Louis

# Excursions in the east

The two main attractions in the east are **Île aux Cerfs** (Stag Island) and the **waterfalls of the Grand Rivière Sud-Est** (Grand River South East). They're both easy to get to and hot favourites with holidaymakers and Mauritian day-trippers. Whether you're staying on the east coast or further afield you can join an organised tour or go independently.

Licensed boat operators make the ten-minute crossing to Île aux Cerfs from the fishing village of **Trou d'Eau Douce** (Hole of Sweet Water). This simple fishing village, on the east coast, has a tourist office, fine beach and parking area. An organised trip through your hotel rep includes all transfers, a tasty barbecue lunch followed by swimming at Île aux Cerfs and a trip to see the waterfalls at Grand Rivière Sud-Est. If you're going independently you can pre-book the waterfall trip either at Trou d'Eau Douce or when you arrive on Île aux Cerfs.

## THINGS TO SEE & DO

### Grand Rivière Sud-Est
Go with a reputable operator by speedboat into the deep estuary of the Grand Rivière Sud-Est where waterfalls, from the longest river in Mauritius, tumble over black basalt cliffs. Unless you're sure-footed don't clamber along the slippery, boulder-ridden banks and do look out for young Indian lads who dive from the waterfalls and into the river and insist on being tipped for their efforts. Book through **Île aux Cerfs Watersports** (ⓐ Trou d'Eau Douce ⓣ 251 1136/255 2121 ⓦ www.ileauxcerfs watersports.com ⓔ info@ileauxcerfswatersports.com ⓛ 09.00–16.00 Mon–Sat, closed Sun). This company also offers parasailing, tube and banana boat rides and individual speedboat trips.

### Île aux Cerfs
Whether it's sunbathing on soft, sandy beaches, snorkelling and swimming in the warm bath-like lagoon or taking a leisurely lunch at the thatched-roof restaurant, everyone from grown-ups to little ones can

expect to have a fun day out on this lovely island. You can windsurf, parasail, hire a kayak or pedalo, or wander around souvenir stalls draped with colourful sarongs and snazzy beachwear. The main beach beside the jetty tends to get crowded but there are stacks of quieter beaches if you head north along meandering pathways skirting a magnificent private 18-hole golf course. Lots of operators at Trou d'Eau Douce will get you to the island but do make sure they are properly licensed. A long-established operator is **Bateau Vicky** (ⓐ Trou d'Eau Douce ⓣ 754 5597), which also organises a barbecue lunch on the tiny Île de l'Est opposite Île aux Cerfs.

⬥ Shaded avenue of casuarina trees on Île aux Cerfs

**Undersea Walk**

A great 'dry hair' activity for non-swimmers, who can explore the seabed and its myriad fish in complete safety by donning a large motorcycle-style helmet attached to an air-supply system.

**Aquaventure** ⓐ Coast Road, Belle Mare ⓣ 256 7953/729 7953

## TAKING A BREAK

**Bateau Vicky Café £** This no-frills modern little café is noted for its friendly staff, who serve Creole titbits and other light bites. Tucked behind Bateau Vicky Tour Operator (see previous page), it's a handy refreshment stop before or after visiting Île aux Cerfs. ⓐ Coast Road, Trou d'Eau Douce ⓣ 754 5597/7460 ⓔ bateauvicky@yahoo.com ⓛ 09.00–16.00 daily

**Chez Tino ££** Find quirky décor, a casual atmosphere, friendly service and fantastic food at this popular eatery overlooking the sea. Splash out on grilled lobster or fill up on tasty Creole cuisine which includes spiced chicken and octopus curry. Excursions also available to Île aux Cerfs. ⓐ Trou d'Eau Douce ⓣ 480 2311/256 1768 ⓛ 11.00–22.00 daily, closed Sun eve

**Le Four à Chaud £££** The menu at this upmarket restaurant features fresh seafood and Creole and European fare. Desserts include crêpes Suzette, coconut sorbet and banana flambéed in rum. There's a decent wine list too. ⓐ Coast Road, Trou d'Eau Douce ⓣ 480 1036 ⓛ 11.00–15.00 Mon–Fri & Sun, 18.00–22.00 daily, closed for Sat lunch ⓘ Reservations recommended

**Victoria 1840 Café des Arts £££** Enjoy gourmet cuisine in this faithfully restored sugar mill-cum-workshop and art gallery exhibiting contemporary paintings by French artist Yvette Maniglier. ⓐ Old Sugar Mill, Victoria Road, Trou d'Eau Douce ⓣ 480 0220 ⓔ jocelyngonzalez@intnet.mu ⓛ 19.00–22.00 daily

# Excursions in the south

In the south of Mauritius, remarkable rolling landscapes of sugar cane, the sea-battered cliffs of Gris-Gris and Souillac and the wild, deserted beaches of Pomponette to the east provide a striking contrast to the gentle lagoons of the northwest and are a part of Mauritius not often seen in brochures. Yet the south has its share of picturesque inland excursions and if you're staying at Le Morne or Bel Ombre these are right on your doorstep. You can visit independently but they're just as easy to get to with tour operators or through your hotel if you're based elsewhere.

## THINGS TO SEE & DO

### Bois Chéri Tea Museum and Factory

The central highlands of Mauritius provide the right weather conditions for growing tea, an industry dating back to 1892. Most of the tea is used for local consumption and processed at Bois Chéri, the island's biggest tea producer. This factory produces the famous vanilla-flavoured tea and more recently herbal and green teas. The leaves are still hand-picked and brought to the factory to be processed and packed.

### THE TEA ROUTE

One of the most popular full-day guided excursions, The Tea Route starts at Domaine des Aubineaux, a colonial house in Curepipe built in 1872. The tour continues with a drive through tea plantations, tea-tasting in a hilltop lodge, a visit to a tea factory and finishes with lunch at St Aubin in the south. It can be booked through any tour operator, or through your hotel. Major operators such as Mauritours (☎ 467 9700 🌐 www.mauritours.net), White Sand Tours (☎ 405 5200 🌐 www.whitesandtours.com) or Summertimes (☎ 427 1111 🌐 www.summer-times.com) also feature this tour on their programmes.

The free factory tour, which takes you through a well-laid-out museum, highlights the history of tea in Mauritius and exhibits tea-processing machinery. You can taste different flavoured teas at the Bois Chéri Chalet, a hilltop pavilion giving wonderful views of the south coast.

ⓐ Bois Chéri, Rivière des Anguilles ❶ 507 0216 ❺ 08.30–16.00 Mon–Fri, 08.30–14.30 Sat, closed Sun ❶ Admission charge only for tea tasting at the Chalet

### Domaine des Aubineaux

The house belonged to a tea-planter and is now a museum containing original furniture, paintings and photographs of days gone by.

ⓐ Curepipe ❶ 676 3089 ⓦ www.larouteduthe.mu (French language only) ⓔ lesaintaubin@intnet.mu ❺ 08.30–16.00 Mon–Fri, 08.30–13.30 Sat, closed Sun

⬥ Tea plantations along 'The Tea Route'

● *Rochester Falls*

## Rochester Falls

Taxis will take you through a maze of cane fields to see these unusual waterfalls on the Savanne River, which tumble over upright basalt rocks from a height of 10 m (33 ft). You might see local lads dive into the waters below, expecting to be tipped for their efforts.

ⓐ 5 km (3 miles) inland from Souillac

## St Aubin Colonial House

If you've booked the Tea Route, then lunch and a visit to this lovely 19th-century colonial house is included. Otherwise you can drop in for tea and sit in style on a wide veranda. Wander round the tropical lawned gardens where there are labelled trees and plants and visit the rum distillery and vanilla plantations nearby.

ⓐ St Aubin ❶ 626 1513 Ⓦ www.saintaubin.mu ⓔ lesaintaubin@intnet.mu ❶ 08.30–16.00 Mon–Sat, closed Sun ❶ Lunch reservations essential

## TAKING A BREAK

**Le Batelage ££** This atmospheric restaurant is housed in a converted stone-built warehouse on the banks of the River Savanne. It is a tranquil hideout, ideal for enjoying a quiet drink or snack. A varied menu of Creole and European food is on offer. ⓐ Coast Road, Souillac ❶ 625 6084 ❶ 11.00–20.00 daily ❶ Reservations recommended

**The Hungry Crocodile ££** Family-friendly restaurant in a tranquil setting with some unusual fare. Try crocodile meat in the form of croquettes, curry, fritters or kebabs, or go for salads, sandwiches or Creole staples. ⓐ La Vanille Réserve de Macareignes, Rivière des Anguilles ❶ 626 2503 Ⓦ www.lavanille-reserve.com ⓔ crocpark@intnet.mu ❶ 12.00–16.00 daily

# Excursions in the southwest

It's well worth putting aside a day to explore the lush mountains and forests in the southwest corner of Mauritius. If you're based in the south or west these attractions are within easy reach and you can join an organised excursion with a guide or hire a taxi for the day from your hotel.

Drive into the **Black River Gorges National Park** from Grande Case Noyale on the west coast or via Curepipe (see page 86) in central Mauritius and head for the **visitor centre at Le Petrin** (❶ 471 1128) near Grand Bassin. Hikers can enter the park at another **visitor centre** (❷ on the A3 coast road near Pavillon de Jade restaurant ❶ 464 4053 ❶ 07.00–17.00 Mon–Fri, 09.00–17.00 Sat & Sun). Both provide comprehensive walking-trail maps enabling you to discover picnic areas, forests and dramatic vistas.

## THINGS TO SEE & DO

### L'Arbre du Voyageur

This private estate surrounded by Traveller's Palms offers quad biking, trekking, hunting and horse riding. Drop by for curried boar or venison in the riverside restaurant or stay overnight in one of the simple attractive log chalets.

❷ Mare Longue, 2 km (1¼ miles) north of Le Petrin visitor centre
❶ 291 4748 ❼ www.l-arbre-du-voyageur.com ❶ 10.00–17.00 daily

### Black River Gorges National Park

Covering 6,575 hectares (16,250 acres), this National Park is the habitat of the tropic bird, the cuckoo shrike, the Mauritian blackbird and the recently endangered Mauritius kestrel. At Black River Gorges viewpoint you'll find a car park, snack stalls and heavenly views of ravines unfolding towards the west coast. Watch out for bands of mischievous macaque monkeys!

❷ 8 km (5 miles) southwest of Le Petrin visitor centre

◆ *Chamarel Coloured Earths*

### Chamarel Coloured Earths and waterfalls

The small coffee-growing village of Chamarel is famous for its Coloured Earths – a remarkable landscape of rainbow-coloured ash caused by the uneven cooling of lava millions of years ago. Combine with a visit to the nearby waterfalls, the highest on Mauritius, tumbling from the Rivière du Cap.

ⓐ Chamarel ⓣ 483 8298 ⓛ 06.00–18.00 daily ⓘ Admission charge

### Grand Bassin

This water-filled crater, dotted with colourful temples and shrines, is of major religious significance to the Hindu population, who believe that it is linked to the Ganges. During the annual Maha Shivaratree festival (see page 105) thousands of pilgrims descend on the lake. Nearby is the 32-m (105-ft)-high statue of the Hindu god Shri Mangal Mahadev.

ⓐ 2 km (1¼ miles) east of Le Petrin visitor centre

### Rhumerie de Chamarel

See how rum is made from sugar cane and take a tot of the stuff at this fascinating distillery. The shop sells quality Mauritian-made goods and there's an upmarket restaurant specialising in organic produce grown on the estate.

ⓐ Route Royale, Chamarel ⓣ 483 7980 ⓦ www.rhumeriedechamarel. com ⓛ 09.00–17.30 Mon–Sat, closed Sun ⓘ Admission charge; guided tours

## TAKING A BREAK

**L'Alchimiste £££** Smart and spacious upmarket restaurant giving superb views of the countryside and mountains. It is renowned for its menu of locally reared duck, venison and wild boar, served with organically grown vegetables and followed by dreamy desserts. There's also a fine wine list.

ⓐ Rhumerie de Chamarel, Route Royale, Chamarel ⓣ 483 7980 ⓦ www.rhumeriedechamarel.com ⓛ 11.30–15.00 Mon–Sat, closed Sun ⓘ Reservations recommended; accepts credit cards

The Rhumerie de Chamarel rum distillery

# Curepipe & plateau towns

For a day away from the beach head to the cooler heights of Curepipe and the residential towns situated on the central plateau of the island. In contrast to the surrounding cane-covered landscapes and diminutive mountains, these towns are over-populated, often traffic-choked areas that appear to merge into one, with 21st-century office buildings, higgledy-piggledy town markets and smart shopping malls.

⬥ *One of the more modern areas of Rose Hill*

The main road (known as 'the motorway') from Grand Baie in the north all the way to Mahébourg in the south gives access to Rose Hill/ Beau Bassin, Quatre Bornes, Phoenix, Floréal and Curepipe. But if you don't want the hassle of sitting in traffic jams there are plenty of tour operators providing excursions to Curepipe. These are often combined with a side trip into Black River Gorges (see page 82) via the island's biggest reservoir at Mare aux Vacoas, which looks like a huge inland sea. Alternatively, you can hire a taxi and make up your own itinerary.

## THINGS TO SEE & DO

### Curepipe Botanic Gardens

Green-fingered visitors can enjoy a stroll in these tranquil gardens along paths named after local dignitaries. Established in 1870, the gardens are much smaller than those at Pamplemousses in the north, but are noted for shaded avenues, lakes and lawns where you can spot indigenous trees, including the only surviving specimen of the *Hyophorbe amaricaulis* or hurricane palm.

ⓐ Botanical Gardens Street, Curepipe ⓒ 06.00–18.00 daily

### Curepipe Town Hall & Carnegie Library

The Town Hall, dating back to the 19th century when Curepipe was given municipality status, and the adjacent Carnegie Library, off Elizabeth II Avenue, are wonderful examples of colonial architecture. They overlook pleasant gardens adorned with a bronze statue of Paul and Virginie, who were young lovers, drowned at sea when the *St Geran* was caught in a storm off the east coast in 1744. The tragedy inspired French author Bernardin St Pierre to write his romantic novel *Paul et Virginie* and even today courting couples meet there despite its proximity to the town's chaotic market.

ⓐ Queen Elizabeth II Avenue, Curepipe ⓣ 670 4897 (Town Hall), 670 6733 (Library) ⓒ 09.00–16.00 Mon-Fri, closed Sat & Sun (Town Hall), 09.00–17.00 Mon-Fri, 09.00–15.00 Sat, closed Sun (Library)

## Floréal Square

If you're a shopaholic you can seek out top brands, such as Clédor for designer jewellery, pullovers and T-shirts by Harris Wilson and lambswool, merino and cashmere collections by Floréal Knitwear in this compact modern shopping square. Finish with a drink and snack at the adjacent cafeteria.

ⓐ Floréal Square, Floréal ⓣ 698 7959 ⓛ 09.00–17.00 Mon–Fri, 09.00–13.00 Sat, closed Sun

## Mauritius Glass Gallery

Recycled glass from households, factories and hotels is collected and turned into unique works of art at this glass gallery where you can see local glass-blowers at work. Take time to stop in the showroom where you can buy unusual handmade souvenirs, such as lampshades and decanters, content in the knowledge that you're contributing to an eco-friendly initiative.

ⓐ Phoenix ⓣ 696 3360 ⓔ mgg@intnet.mu ⓛ 08.00–17.00 Mon–Sat, closed Sun

## Rose Hill/Beau Bassin

Rose Hill and Beau Bassin have merged into one town over the years. The main Royal Road is a jumble of shops with crowded pavements where street hawkers sell just about anything at knock-down prices. For an atmospheric local scene head to the market groaning with fruit and vegetables or snap up bargain T-shirts, sarongs, baskets, beachwear and souvenirs in the covered stalls nearby.

## Trou aux Cerfs

This extinct crater, a 15-minute taxi ride northwest of Curepipe, was formed millions of years ago as a result of volcanic activity. At 650 m (2,133 ft) above sea level, the views of mountains, towns and coast, particularly on a clear day, are quite spectacular. You can walk round the perimeter in complete safety peering into the depths, now filled with water and dense vegetation.

## TAKING A BREAK

**Café de Paris £** Relax at this watering hole selling coffee, sandwiches, baguettes, pizza and salads after tramping round the arcades of Curepipe. Sit at shaded tables on the first-floor terrace with views of the town. ⓐ Galeries des Îles, Chasteauneuf Road, Curepipe ⓣ 676 2216 ⓛ 09.00–16.00 Mon–Sat, closed Sun

**Foodcourt £** For a break from shopping try this self-service foodcourt, which has outlets serving everything from tandoori, Indian, Creole and Chinese to burgers, cakes, pastries and snacks. Eat inside or at the picnic benches outside. ⓐ Trianon Shopping Park, near Quatre Bornes ⓛ 10.00–20.00 Mon–Sat, 10.00–13.00 Sun

**Mokafé £** Enjoy smoked marlin baguettes, pizzas and salads in this charming French-style café after shopping at Trianon. ⓐ Trianon Shopping Park, near Quatre Bornes ⓣ 464 4996 ⓛ 09.00–16.00 Mon–Sat, closed Sun

**Le Pekinois £** Simple Chinese restaurant that's been going for years, noted for fast, efficient service and a menu featuring fried noodles, rice, seafood, pork and vegetable dishes. ⓐ Corner of Royal Road and Ambrose Street, Rose Hill ⓣ 454 7229 ⓛ 11.00–20.00 Mon–Sat, closed Sun

**Café Baudelaire ££** Contemporary-style eatery shaded by banyan trees inside the Institut Français. Ideal for snacks or more substantial fare prepared under the aegis of French chef Patrice Dumont. ⓐ 30 Avenue Julius Nyerere, Rose Hill ⓣ 465 7109 ⓔ admin@dumont.mu ⓛ 11.00–15.00 Mon–Sat, closed Sun

**Ginger ££** Fusion cuisine served at this sophisticated and elegant restaurant in the heart of the town. ⓐ Garden Village Centre, Sir Winston Churchill Street, Curepipe ⓣ 670 0250 ⓛ 09.00–22.00 Mon–Sat, closed Sun & public holidays

**Happy Rajah ££** The best place in town for authentic Indian food prepared by chefs from Delhi served up in a restored colonial-style house. This 90-seat restaurant has an indoor section and airy veranda. ⓐ St Jean Road, Quatre Bornes ① 427 1854/257 3877 ⓦ www.happyrajah.com ⓔ info@happyrajah.com ① 12.00–14.30, 18.30–22.30 Mon–Sat, closed Sun

**Mon Repos ££** This atmospheric 150-year-old colonial house has a décor of antique furniture and is set in tropical gardens. For a leisurely lunch sit on the veranda or in the gardens and dine on house specialities like octopus salad and curries served with traditional pickles. ⓐ Belzim Estate, Trianon ① 467 6437/465 8403 ⓦ www.monrepos.mu ⓔ contact@monrepos.mu ① 11.30–15.30 Mon–Sat, closed Sun ① Dinner on reservation

**La Potinière ££** The cosy, warm and casual décor and friendly service attract a repeat clientele for Mauritian specialities, including seafood, game and heart of palm salad. ⓐ Sir Winston Churchill Street, Curepipe ① 670 2648 ⓦ http://lapotiniere.net ⓔ potiniere@intnet.mu ① 10.00–15.00, 18.30–22.00 Tues–Sat, closed Sun & Mon

**L'Atelier Dumont £££** First-class service, Mediterranean cuisine and great wine at this high-end restaurant. Try the grilled *babonne* (spotted coral grouper) and their unforgettable chocolate gâteau. ⓐ 1 Cyber City, Ebene ① 467 2546 ⓔ patrice@dumont.mu ① 08.00–17.00 Mon & Tues, 08.00–24.00 Wed–Sat, closed Sun

**Domaine des 7 Vallées £££** Beautiful country location south of Curepipe, which also offers deer hunting, quad biking and cycling. Specialities include venison and game served with home-made chutneys in a rustic colonial-style pavilion-cum-hunting lodge. ⓐ Rue Lapeyre, Nouvelle France ① 631 3336 ⓦ www.domainedes7vallees.com ① 10.00–16.00 daily ① Open evenings on reservation only for groups of 10 or more

⏵ *A traditional market shop*

LIFESTYLE
Island life

# Food & drink

Eating in Mauritius is like going on a one-stop international food tour. The diversity of the food reflects the multiculturalism of the nation. The food that you'll come across can be characteristically spicy, fragrantly flavoured, deliciously aromatic and, depending on where you go, decidedly sophisticated. Grand Baie, Flic en Flac and Port Louis are the places for international dining in grand surroundings and it's wise to make a reservation, especially on Friday and Saturday nights.

While many hotel restaurants provide excellent buffets and à la carte dining, eating out is not expensive and it's worth trying the local cuisine even if you are on an all-inclusive package. Tipping is not obligatory, but always appreciated for good service. Remember that 15 per cent VAT is added to your bill and in some cases the service charge may already be included.

⬥ *A typical spread of Mauritian delicacies*

Mauritians tend to break early for lunch at around 11.30, filling up on a baguette or *dholl puri* (lentil pancake) or having a one-course meal at a restaurant. Restaurants are open for dinner typically from 18.00 to around 22.00 during the week and often stay open later on a Friday and Saturday.

## LOCAL RESTAURANTS

Creole, Chinese and European food all feature on a typical restaurant menu. Creole food is a term encompassing local food, which can include Indian-style curries and French-influenced casseroles and stews known as *rougailles* and *daubes*, which are often served with mounds of white rice or noodles and accompanied by spicy chilli paste and chutneys. Portions are generous, making a three-course meal a bit over the top unless you're really famished.

Mauritians constantly nibble on tasty little deep-fried snacks bought from street vendors. Among the favourites, which also feature on most menus, are meat, fish or vegetable fritters, *dholl puris*, *gateaux piments* (chilli cakes), *samousas* and quartered sweet pineapples doused in chilli sauce.

## FISH

If you're in the mood for fish, try the local smoked marlin served with a wedge of lemon as a starter and follow with a main course of the firm-fleshed local fish, such as tuna, *cordonnier* (surgeon fish), *capitaine* (white snapper) or *vieille rouge* (grouper), or opt for the more expensive lobster, which is sold by weight, along with prawns and octopus grilled or curried to perfection. A Rodriguan speciality is *cono-cono*, an over-sized type of whelk, served in a refreshing salad.

## MEAT

The best beef and lamb is imported from South Africa and Australia and turns up as melt-in-the-mouth steaks. The local pork and chicken are also good, especially in Chinese cuisine. It is also worth trying some unusual meats that would be expensive at home, such as *carri cerf* (venison curry) and *cochon marron* (wild boar curry).

## VEGETARIAN FOOD

Vegetarians will find a cornucopia of produce, from the more unfamiliar *brèdes* (leafy spinach-like greens) and *petsai* (Chinese pak choi) to members of the marrow family under the Creole names of *pipengaille*, *patisson* and *giraumon*. *Lalo* (okra) is a popular vegetable and is delicious turned into a curry or in a salad. Pulses come as *gros pois* (butter beans), *haricots rouges* (red beans) and *dholl* (lentils) served on their own or as an accompaniment to rice and vegetable curry. A must-try is *coeur de palmiste* (heart of palm), also known as Millionaire's Salad.

Tropical fruits abound with fat lychees, sweet pawpaws, watermelons and mangos in the summer months, grenadines, pineapples and bananas year round, plus custard apples, guavas, strawberries, football-sized pomelos (a kind of grapefruit) and crisp grapes, apples and pears from South Africa.

## DESSERTS & SWEETS

In hotel restaurants desserts from all over the world tempt the sweet-toothed. In outside restaurants these tend to be confined to crêpes (pancakes) or fresh fruit, depending on the season, served with a selection of ice cream or sorbet. There are some unusual cakes and pastries, which you can buy in patisseries and supermarkets. Mauritian favourites include the small pink-iced biscuits called *napolitaines* and small squares of bread, coconut and maize pudding. During Chinese New Year you can find waxy little cakes called *gateaux cirés*. Indian sweetmeats available year round include highly sugared confections such as *gulab jamun* or *gateau moutail* (syrupy doughnuts with cardamom), *besan ladoo* (gram-flour balls) and *rasgoulas* (sweet powdered-milk balls). A traditional Indian dessert, served after a meal, is *kulfi*, a pistachio and almond ice cream, made with evaporated milk.

## DRINKS

Imported drink attracts heavy taxes. Supermarkets stock fruit juices, fizzy drinks, bottled water, and wines and spirits from many countries. The local beer to go for is Phoenix but the stronger Blue Marlin and Black

Eagle are also popular. Rum is also produced locally and the best brand is Green Island, served neat or in a cocktail.

Tea can come plain or vanilla-flavoured and there are dozens of infusions or herb-flavoured teas, which are good after a meal. Hotels and most restaurants serve a good range of coffee, from the local Chamarel to more familiar cappuccino and espresso.

◆ *Enjoy the weather and dine alfresco*

# Menu decoder

## SNACKS & STARTERS

**Croquettes de poulet/ourite/crevette** Spicy chicken/octopus/prawn fritters

**Dholl puris** Large crushed lentil pancakes filled with vegetables

**Gateaux piments** Deep-fried spicy bites made from crushed lentils and chilli

**Hakien** Chinese spring roll filled with vegetables or pork

**Marlin fumé** Smoked marlin served in thin slices not unlike smoked salmon

**Salade ourite** Octopus salad

**Salade palmiste/Coeur de palmiste** Often known as Millionaire's Salad this is a light starter made from grated heart of palm

**Samousas** Deep-fried triangular pastries filled with curry or vegetables

## SAUCES, PICKLES & CHUTNEYS

**Achard de legumes** Light vegetable pickle not unlike piccalilli, flavoured with turmeric, garlic and spices

**Chatini coco** Grated coconut chutney mixed with mint, chilli and tamarind

**Chatini pommes d'amour** Spicy tomato chutney with chopped onion, coriander and chilli

**Mangues confits** Thinly sliced green mangos marinated in turmeric, fenugreek, chilli and mustard oil

**Piments ecrasés** A smooth paste made from crushed green or red chillis, ginger, vinegar and oil

**Sauce ail** A thin sauce made from vinegar, honey and garlic

## CURRIES

**Carri cerf** Venison curry

**Carri ourite** Octopus curry

**Carri poisson** Fish curry

**Carri poulet et crevettes** Mixed chicken and prawn curry

**Cochon marron** Wild boar curry

**Vindaye poisson** Fish vindaloo

## BREAD

Indian breads to eat with curries include naan, *farathas* and *puris*. These are lighter and smaller than their gut-busting cousins, *dholl puris*.

## RICE & NOODLES

**Bol renversé** Spicy rice with pork, chicken and spicy sausage layered with a fried egg and *brèdes* (greens) served upside down from a bowl

**Briyani** A rice dish made with fish, beef or venison

**Fooyang** Filling type of omelette folded in half like a pancake and filled with seafood

**Meefoon** Vermicelli-like noodles

**Mines frites** Fried noodles with a mixture of seafood, chicken and meat

## MEAT

**Char Siu** Chinese-style roast pork

**Daube de poulet** Casseroled chicken in rich tomato and herb wine sauce

**Rougaille de saucisses** Sausages in rich tomato, onion, ginger and garlic sauce flavoured with parsley and thyme

**Steak au poivre** Pepper steak

## VEGETABLES

**Brèdes** Boiled leafy greens

**Carri dholl** Yellow split pea curry

**Gratin de giraumon** Pumpkin gratin

**Gros pois** Giant butter beans/lima beans

## FISH & SEAFOOD

**Boulettes poisson** Steamed fish balls

**Daube ourite** Casseroled octopus in rich tomato and herb sauce

**Poisson aigre doux** Chinese-style sweet-and-sour filleted white fish

**Poisson gingembre** Chinese-style fish cooked whole or sliced in a ginger sauce

**Poisson salé** Fried salt fish served with onions

## DESSERTS

**Bananes braiseés** Bananas braised in sugar and butter

**Kulfi** Indian ice cream made from evaporated milk, pistachios and almonds

**Poutou** Steamed ground rice cakes served during Chinese celebrations

**Tarte banane** Banana tart

## DRINKS

**Alouda** A Port Louis market special made from milk, water, crushed ice, vanilla essence, sugar and basil seeds

**Infusion** Herbal tea drunk after a meal to aid digestion

**Lassi** Refreshing yoghurt and water drink

# Shopping

Malls and markets are the best places for tracking down local souvenirs, such as woven raffia bags, herbs, spices, T-shirts and beachwear. Prices in shops tend to be fixed, although you might get a small discount if you make several purchases. To test your bargaining skills head to Port Louis' central market in Queen Street. Some shops advertise Duty Free shopping, which in effect means you don't pay VAT. However, don't expect to find any real bargains when it comes to buying imported or branded goods.

Tour operators organise shopping excursions to Curepipe for its Chinese shops specialising in silk and porcelain, and to Floréal for locally produced knitwear, including cashmere and cotton. Trianon and Orchard Shopping Centres in Quatre Bornes and Les Halles in Phoenix offer a more local scene.

## CAUDAN WATERFRONT

Dozens of modern shops, restaurants and cafés in this pedestrian area of Port Louis will keep the whole family occupied for the day. The craft market here contains two floors of colourful stalls where you can buy local goods and watch craftspeople at work. Look out for jewellery, recycled glass ornaments, embroidered tablecloths and bedspreads, saris, beachwear, paintings, dolls, toys and dodo souvenirs. More unusual buys to look for are gift packets of herbs, spices, tea, coffee and sugar.

ⓐ Caudan Waterfront, Port Louis ❶ 211 6560 Ⓦ www.caudan.com
🕒 09.30–17.30 Mon–Sat, closed Sun

## GRAND BAIE

Grand Baie's top shopping spots are the outlets at **Sunset Boulevard** and **Grand Baie Store Plaza** (both on the coast road) for smart casual clothing, home accessories and beachwear. **Super U** complex (ⓐ Richmond Hill) is good for everyday supermarket goods and **Grand Baie Bazaar** (ⓐ Racket Road) has 120 stalls of handicrafts and clothing at knock-down prices.

## RUISSEAU CREOLE

Shops selling designer clothing and accessories, handicrafts, tableware, antiques, model ships and works of art are just some of the specialist outlets at this upmarket shopping centre on the west coast.

ⓐ La Mivoie, Black River ⓣ 483 8000 ⓦ www.ruisseaucreole.com
ⓒ 09.30–18.30 Mon–Sat, closed Sun

## LOCAL ART GALLERIES

You can buy unusual framed or unframed paintings by local artists. These wildly colourful works, depicting unique Mauritian scenes, can be viewed and purchased at:

**Galerie du Moulin Cassé** ⓐ Old Mill Road, Pereybère
ⓣ 727 0672/263 0672

**Galerie Hélène de Senneville** ⓐ Royal Road, Pointe aux Canonniers
ⓣ 263 7426

**Galerie Vaco Baissac** ⓐ Dodo Square, Grand Baie ⓣ 263 3106

△ Find unusual artworks in Mauritius' many galleries

# Children

Mauritius is very much a family destination and children are welcome everywhere. The larger hotels have excellent mini-clubs to keep them entertained and non-hotel restaurants are becoming more child-friendly and will supply high chairs. Many feature children's menus but if they don't the owner will be only too happy to knock up smaller portions or leave out ingredients like chilli or garlic in certain meals.

Playing around on the beach or gazing at corals from a glass-bottom boat are favourites with smaller children. For a change of scenery with animals and nature as part of the deal, head to **Casela Nature and Leisure Park** (see page 44), **La Vanille Réserve des Mascareignes** (see page 36), take in tropical flora at the **Sir Seewoosagur Ramgoolam Botanic Gardens** (see page 53) or get up close to giant **Aldabra tortoises on Rodrigues** (see pages 60–62). For older children with a sense of adventure, there are a host of adrenalin-charged sports and activities on

⬤ *Feeding time at Casela Nature and Leisure Park*

offer. For the curious, there are some interesting museums too. Most attractions have reduced admission charges for children and families.

## RAJIV GANDHI SCIENCE CENTRE

Explore Mauritian geography, natural resources, people and climate at this modern, well-laid-out museum. Meet local schoolchildren in the Fun Science section where rolling balls, pendulums, strange liquids and magnets provide hours of educational and interactive fun.

ⓐ Old Moka Road, Bell Village, Port Louis ⓣ 213 2773 ⓦ www.gov.mu/portal/site/rajiv ⓛ 09.00–16.30 daily ⓘ Admission charge

## WALKING WITH LIONS AND CHEETAHS

Julie and Graeme Bristow, parents of a young family themselves, are owners of a pride of lions and cheetahs at **Casela Nature and Leisure Park** and are all too aware of the safety issues when it comes to interaction with big cats. Young children can view the animals from a safety platform and learn all about their habits. Older visitors are fully briefed before walking with these magnificent creatures in the wild under Graeme's expert supervision. Don't forget your camera and wear comfortable trainers.

ⓐ Casela Nature and Leisure Park, Cascavelle ⓣ 452 5546 ⓕ 452 5574 ⓦ www.safari-adventures-mauritius.com ⓔ safari-adventures@intnet.mu ⓛ 09.00–17.00 daily, viewings only Sun, closed Christmas Day, Boxing Day & New Year's Day ⓘ Admission charge; height and age restrictions apply; booking advised

## QUAD BIKING

Quad biking is very popular with older children. Gloves, helmets and goggles are provided. The best places for this are at **Ferney Valley** and **Domaine de l'Étoile** (see page 32), **Domaine des 7 Vallées** (see page 90), **Casela Nature and Leisure Park** (see page 44) and **Wild Things Adventure** (ⓐ Mon Choisy, Grand Baie near the petrol station ⓣ 933 2835 ⓔ wildthingmu@gmail.com ⓛ 10.00–16.00 daily ⓘ Booking advised).

# Sports & activities

### BIG GAME FISHING

**Sofitel Imperial Hotel** ⓐ Wolmar, Flic en Flac ⓣ 453 8700 ⓦ www.
sofitel.com ⓔ H144@sofitel.com
**Corsaire Club** ⓐ Trou aux Biches ⓣ 265 5209
**JP Henry Charters** ⓐ Black River ⓣ 729 0901 ⓕ 483 5038
ⓦ www.blackriver-mauritius.com ⓔ info@blackriver-mauritius.com
**Le Morne Anglers Club** ⓐ Black River ⓣ 483 5801 ⓦ www.morne
anglers.com ⓔ lmaclub@intnet.mu
**La Pirogue Big Game** ⓐ Wolmar ⓣ 453 8054 ⓦ www.lapirogue
biggame.com

● *Watersports are very popular on Mauritius*

## CRUISING

Cruising along the coast or to the offshore islands is a year-round activity. A reputable tour company is **Summertimes** (☎ 427 1111 🌐 www.summer-times.com); they can arrange day excursions with lunch on catamarans from Grand Baie in the north, from the east coast and from Black River Yacht Club on the west coast.

## CYCLING

You can hire a bike from your hotel or from individual operators but do check that the brakes work properly. The safest way is to ride in convoy with a guide from your hotel. Ask your hotel rep for details.

## DIVING

There are dozens of PADI-approved diving schools and many are attached to hotels. Top names include:

**Blue Water Diving Center** ⓐ Mon Choisy, Grand Baie ☎ 265 6700 🟠 265 7186 🌐 www.bluewaterdivingcenter.com ⓔ info.bluewater@ intnet.mu 🕒 08.30–16.30 Mon–Sat, closed Sun & public holidays 🛈 Reservations only; nitrox-equipped

**Diving Mon Plaisir** ⓐ Villas Mon Plaisir, Point aux Piments ☎ 261 7980 🌐 www.villasmonplaisir.com

**Shandrani Hotel** has a PADI National Geographic diving centre, sailing club and kite-surfing school. ⓐ Le Chaland, Blue Bay ☎ 603 4343 🌐 www.shandrani-hotel.com

## GOLF

There are many golfing opportunities on Mauritius, often on courses with spectacular views. Popular 18-hole courses include **Anahita** (ⓐ Deep River, Beau Champs, GRSE ☎ 402 2200 🌐 www.anahita.mu), **Golf du Château** (ⓐ Val Riche Nature Reserve, Bel Ombre ☎ 623 5600 🌐 www.domainedebelombre.mu), **Legends** and **Links** (ⓐ Constance Belle Mare Plage Hotel ☎ 402 2600 🌐 www.bellemareplagehotel.com), **Paradis** (ⓐ Paradis Hotel ☎ 401 5050 🌐 www.paradis-hotel.com), **Le Touessrok** on Île aux Cerfs (ⓐ Touessrok Hotel, Trou d'Eau Douce

🕓 402 7400 Ⓦ www.letouessrokresort.com) and **Tamarina** (🅐 Tamarin Bay 🕓 401 3006 Ⓦ www.tamarina.mu). There are 9-hole golf courses at Maritim Hotel in the north, St Geran Hotel in the east, Shandrani Hotel in the south and Sofitel in the west.

## HIKING & EXTREME SPORTS
For nature walks, hiking, trekking, abseiling and rock climbing contact:
**Casela Yemen Nature Escapade** 🅐 Cascavelles 🕓 452 2828
Ⓦ www.caselayemen.mu
**Chazal** 🅐 Chamonix 🕓 622 7234 or 422 3117 🕓 697 2160
**Ciel et Nature** 🕓 433 1050 Ⓦ www.cieletnature.com
**Vertical World** 🅐 Curepipe 🕓 251 1107 or 697 5430
Ⓦ www.verticalworldltd.com
**Yanature** 🅐 Black River 🕓 785 6177 Ⓦ www.trekkingilemaurice.com

## HORSE RIDING
**Domaine Les Pailles** 🅐 Les Guibies, Pailles 🕓 286 4225
Ⓦ www.domainelespailles.net 🅔 domaine.sales@intnet.mu
**Vieille Cheminée** 🅐 Chamarel 🕓 483 5249 or 725 5546
Ⓦ www.lavieillecheminee.com 🅔 caroline@lavieillecheminee.com

# Festivals & events

The multiculturalism of Mauritius is reflected in its many different festivals. Many religious festivals are movable dates and sporting and cultural events are scheduled nearer the time, so it's best to contact the tourist office or visit Ⓦ www.tourism-mauritius.mu for full details.

## JANUARY/FEBRUARY
### Thaipoosum Cavadee
This religious festival celebrated by the Tamil community is not for the squeamish. Devotees pierce their bodies and faces with needles in an act of penance and then carry the *cavadee* (a small wooden arch adorned with flowers) containing a pot of milk through the streets to the temple where it is placed before the warrior god, Muruga.

### Chinese New Year (also known as the Chinese Spring Festival)
Throughout the day and well into the night the Chinese community let off firecrackers to drive away evil spirits. Port Louis' Chinatown draws large crowds for boisterous displays of lion dancing and free cultural and music events. Restaurants and shops are open until midnight, food stalls line the streets and gifts wrapped in red, the colour of happiness, are distributed among friends and family.

## FEBRUARY/MARCH
### Maha Shivaratree
This major Hindu festival is attended by thousands of devotees in honour of Lord Shiva. Pilgrims dressed in white and bearing *kanwars* (large wooden arches covered with flowers) walk from all over the island to Grand Bassin to pray and bathe in the waters they believe to be linked to the Ganges.

### Holi
Hindu families burn effigies of the evil demon Holika before letting their hair down in a two-day ritual of good luck when coloured water and powder is squirted over anything that moves, including passers-by!

◯ *Tamil devotee celebrates Thaipoosum Cavadee*

### Independence/Republic Day

Celebrations to mark Mauritius' independence from Britain in 1968 and becoming a Commonwealth republic in 1992 are held all over the island with public buildings draped in the national flag. Political speeches and cultural shows are held mainly in Port Louis and Mahébourg. 🕐 12 Mar

## MARCH/APRIL

### Ougadi

This low-key festival celebrates the Hindu Telegu New Year. Sometimes there will be a cultural show and during this time traditional cakes are distributed among friends and neighbours.

## AUGUST/SEPTEMBER

### Assumption Day

Roman Catholics attend Mass on this day, with the largest held at Marie Reine de la Paix in Port Louis. Big celebrations also take place in Rodrigues at the statue of La Reine de Rodrigues outside Port Mathurin. 🕐 15 Aug

### Ganesh Chaturthi

Followers commemorate the birth of Ganesh, the Hindu god of wisdom, by immersing effigies in the sea or along riverbanks on the fourth day of the lunar month in August or September.

### Père Laval

Père Laval, a French missionary who came to Mauritius in the 19th century, was believed to have special healing powers. He was buried at Saint Croix church to the north of Port Louis and every year thousands of pilgrims converge at his tomb to pray. 🕐 9 Sept

## SEPTEMBER/OCTOBER

### Eid ul-Fitr

This three-day festival marks the end of Ramadan, a one-month period of fasting for the Muslim community, when gifts and food are given to the poor and needy. It's very much a family occasion and the exact date depends on the sighting of the moon.

## OCTOBER/NOVEMBER
### Divali or Festival of Lights
During this major festival, Hindus light up their gardens and houses with candles placed in small clay pots, special cakes are made, and prayers are offered in a celebration of good triumphing over evil. Take in the local atmosphere by strolling in the streets of Triolet.

## NOVEMBER
### Mahébourg Regatta
Some 30 *pirogues* (traditional sailing boats) take part in this three-day regatta, which takes place in the lagoon at Mahébourg in an atmosphere of Creole jollity.  www.laregatta.com

## DECEMBER
### International Creole Festival
This colourful festival is a newcomer to the events scene with a week-long programme of all-night concerts and performances by Creole artists from Mauritius and the Indian Ocean region.

## CALENDAR OF OTHER OFFICIAL RELIGIOUS & PUBLIC HOLIDAYS
**1 & 2 January** New Year
**1 February** Abolition of Slavery Day
**1 May** Labour Day
**1 November** All Saints' Day
**2 November** First Labourers' Day
**25 December** Christmas Day

---

▶ *A sign points visitors to the Coloured Earths at Chamarel*

TERRES DE
7 COULEURS
← 1.6km

# PRACTICAL INFORMATION
Tips & advice

# Accommodation

This price guide is based on a double room per night including breakfast:
£ under R5,000   ££ R5,000–R10,000   £££ over R10,000

### BALACLAVA

**Grand Mauritian £££** Spacious 193-room hotel with stylish décor. Two bars, three restaurants and large pool are all on one level with spa, state-of-the-art gym and kids' club, plus everything you'd expect in a resort hotel. ⓐ Turtle Bay ⓣ 204 1400 ⓦ www.thegrandmauritian.com

### BEL OMBRE

**Telfair £££** Grand colonial-style hotel reflecting times past combined with modern luxury and amenities. Choose from five restaurants, including the Château de Bel Ombre overlooking the hotel's golf course, spoil yourself in the spa or hike in Valriche Forest nearby. ⓐ Bel Ombre ⓣ 601 5500 ⓦ www.heritageletelfair.mu

### BELLE MARE

**Constance Belle Mare Plage £££** Contemporary décor blends with tradition in the villas, rooms and suites of this spacious hotel. With two golf courses, great beach and sports facilities, ten restaurants and bars, kids' club and beauty treatments, there's more than enough to keep everyone entertained. ⓐ Coast Road, Belle Mare ⓣ 402 2777 ⓦ www.bellemareplagehotel.com

### FLIC EN FLAC

**Tamarin £** Informal yet elegant 59-room hotel with large pool and views of Tamarin Mountain, a lively restaurant and jazz nights. ⓐ Tamarin Beach ⓣ 483 6927 ⓦ www.hoteltamarin.com

### GRAND BAIE

**Veranda ££** Sweeping views of the bay and direct access to the beach attract families and couples. Spa and daily entertainment, kids' club and free watersports all within walking distance of shops, bars and restaurants. ❸ Royal Road ❶ 209 8000 ❽ www.veranda-resorts.com

### GRAND GAUBE

**Paul & Virginie ££** Boutique-style ambience beside the sea, ideal for couples seeking romantic escape. Lovely open-sided bar, two pools, buffet restaurant and stylish seafood restaurant. ❸ Coast Road ❶ 288 0215 ❽ www.veranda-resorts.com

### MAHÉBOURG

**Blue Lagoon Beach Hotel £** Simple family hotel with 72 rooms, ideal for exploring Blue Bay Marine Park and with nightly themed buffets and entertainment. The boathouse offers a good range of watersports. ❸ Blue Bay ❶ 631 9046 ❽ www.bluelagoonbeachhotel.com

### LE MORNE

**Indian Resort £££** Big-scale luxury on an immense beach, with nine restaurants and bars, two pools plus kids' pool, health and beauty centre, a kite-surfing school plus free watersports. ❸ Le Morne ❶ 261 8000 ❽ www.apavou-hotels.com

### PEREYBÈRE

**Hibiscus ££** This charming small hotel offers value for money, especially considering its fine beach location and proximity to shops and bars. Pleasant restaurants with live music, beach bar, spa and kids' club. ❸ Royal Road ❶ 263 8554 ❽ www.hibiscushotel.com

### RODRIGUES

**Mourouk Ebony £** Attractive bungalow accommodation and luxury suites strung across a cliff top with panoramic ocean views. Rustic-style restaurant, daily entertainment and kids' club, plus windsurfing and diving school. ❸ Pâté Reynieux, Port Sud-Est ❶ 832 3351 ❽ www.mouroukebonyhotel.com

# Preparing to go

## GETTING THERE

Most visitors arrive in Mauritius on a package holiday from London Heathrow with the national airline, Air Mauritius (☎ 020 7434 4375 ⓦ www.airmauritius.com). Other airlines include British Airways (ⓦ www.ba.com) and Air France (ⓦ www.airfrance.co.uk) via Paris. The direct flight from London takes approximately 11 hours. All-inclusive or half-board packages from budget right through to luxury accommodation can be booked through a number of UK operators.

Many people are aware that air travel emits $CO_2$, which contributes to climate change. You may be interested in the possibility of lessening the environmental impact of your flight through the charity **Climate Care**, which offsets your $CO_2$ by funding environmental projects around the world. Visit ⓦ www.jpmorganclimatecare.com

## TOURISM AUTHORITY

Mauritius Tourism Promotion Authority ⓐ 32–33 Elvaston Place, London SW7 5NW ☎ 020 7584 3666 ⓦ www.tourism-mauritius.mu ⓔ mtpa@btinternet.com

## BEFORE YOU LEAVE

Mauritius poses no serious health risks; the country is free from malaria, yellow fever, cholera and other tropical diseases. No vaccination certificates are required unless you have travelled through a country with a yellow fever risk within the six days preceding your arrival.

### TRAVEL INSURANCE

Travel insurance is always a good idea if only to take away the stress of knowing that any expenses should be met if you are injured or fall ill. Always read the small print and make sure the cover is adequate for your particular needs.

Bring light cotton clothing, which is ideal for tropical and humid conditions, and if you're holidaying during the cooler months of May to September take a light cardigan or pashmina for chilly evenings. Men need not bother with a dinner suit and tie since after dark the emphasis is on smart-casual wear. Pack hats, sunglasses and a high-factor sunblock, mosquito repellent and a pocket torch because roads are poorly lit at night. If you plan on trekking take sturdy shoes, and if you're on any special medication make sure you have enough for your stay.

## ENTRY FORMALITIES

No visas are needed for EU nationals and citizens of the USA and all Commonwealth countries. Entry is normally granted for the duration of your stay or up to a maximum of three months. You must have a passport that is valid for at least six months on the date you leave Mauritius, a return or onward ticket, proof of accommodation including contact details, and proof you have enough funds for your stay. For an extension of stay, contact **Passport and Immigration Office** ⓐ Sterling House, 9–11 Lislet Geoffroy Street, Port Louis ⓣ 210 9312 ⓕ 210 9322 ⓔ piomain@mail.gov.mu.

You can import the following items duty-free: 250 g of tobacco (including cigarettes and cigars), 1 litre of spirits, 2 litres of wine, ale or beer.

You are allowed to bring in prescription medicines for personal use and you should keep these in a separate container, complete with a copy of the prescription, to produce at customs if necessary. However, remember that drug trafficking carries severe penalties.

## MONEY

The currency used in Mauritius is the Mauritius Rupee (MR) although increasingly hotels and some restaurants quote in euros. Major credit cards, such as MasterCard/Access and Visa are accepted in most places but always check first. There are plenty of banks, ATM facilities and bureaux de change in Port Louis, Grand Baie, Flic en Flac and around the island generally, including the airport. Currency is provided in local Mauritius Rupees.

**CYCLONES**

The official cyclone season is from November to April. Weather stations track their routes and cyclone warnings are given days in advance. Most cyclones pass by but others can wreak havoc on the local people. Hotels are well geared up to deal with cyclones and you're unlikely to be affected.

## CLIMATE

Mauritius is a year-round destination for water-lovers and sun-seekers, with just two seasons – summer and winter. During summer, from November to April, the mercury rises to 35°C (95°F) bringing hot and humid conditions and short bursts of heavy rainfall. In winter, from May to October, there tends to be less rain and temperatures are more comfortable at around 25°C (77°F) with a drop in temperature at night. Southeast trade winds blow all year round, bringing cooling breezes to the south and east coasts during the hot summer, but in winter these winds can be quite uncomfortable.

The best time for diving is from November to March when underwater visibility is particularly good. If you're hiking, avoid November to April when paths are slippery and it is also very hot. The best time for big-game fishing is from October to April.

## BAGGAGE ALLOWANCE

Baggage allowances vary from airline to airline and your free allowance is shown on your ticket. The international baggage allowance for Air Mauritius is 23 kg (50 lbs) per person in economy class and 30 kg (66 lbs) in Business Class. The maximum weight per individual piece of checked baggage must not exceed 23 kg (50 lbs). If you are flying to Rodrigues your luggage is limited to 15 kg (33 lbs). Cabin baggage must not weigh more than 7 kg (15 lbs) and must conform to cabin size. For further information visit Ⓦ www.airmauritius.com

# During your stay

## AIRPORTS

Sir Seewoosagur Ramgoolam International Airport, often abbreviated to SSR (☎ 603 6000 🌐 http://aml.mru.aero), is located at Plaisance in the southeast of Mauritius, approximately 48 km (30 miles) south of the capital, Port Louis. You're unlikely to encounter any hassle at immigration, although if several flights arrive together there may be long queues. The airport is a non-smoking area. There are duty-free shops and public telephones in both the arrivals and departures terminals.

In the arrivals hall you can change money at Thomas Cook and at bank counters, including Barclays; alternatively, use the ATM machine immediately outside. There is a Tourist Information Counter, an AHRIM (Association of Hoteliers and Restaurants in Mauritius) Counter where you can book accommodation, and car-rental agencies. Your holiday rep will normally wait at the top of a ramped walkway outside the arrivals building for your onward transfer.

There is no bus service at the airport but there is a pay car park for 600 vehicles. Taxi drivers will tout for your custom as soon as you emerge from the terminal. Taxis are metered but drivers rarely use them so you should always agree a fare before accepting a ride and don't be afraid to negotiate. As a general rule of thumb, expect to pay anything between R1,275–R1,550 if you're going to the north, around R1,600 for the east and between R1,300–R1,600 for the south and west. A useful website is 🌐 www.taxicabmauritius.com

Rodrigues' airport is Sir Gaetan Duval (☎ 832 7888) at Plaine Corail in the southwest of the island. Facilities include free parking, cafeteria, souvenir shop, telephone services, and bus and taxi transport.

## COMMUNICATIONS

Avoid using your hotel telephone as charges can be excessive. You can make cheap international calls at public payphones using the pre-paid Sezam, Passe Partout or MTML Cards. The cards are available in denominations of R75, R150 and R250 (excluding VAT) from many outlets.

If you have a mobile phone the easiest and cheapest way to keep in touch is to buy a pre-paid starter pack and SIM card from the local network, Orange. Top-up cards in denominations of R50, R100 and R300 (excluding VAT) can be bought from outlets displaying the Orange logo. For further information visit Ⓦ www.orange.mu

**TELEPHONING MAURITIUS**
From Europe: 00 + 230 + number
From US and Canada: 011 + 230 + number
From Australia: 0011 + 230 + number
From New Zealand: 00 + 230 + number
From South Africa: 00 + 230 + number

**TELEPHONING FROM MAURITIUS**
To the UK: 020 + 44 + number
To the US and Canada: 020 + 1 + number
To Australia: 020 + 61 + number
To New Zealand: 020 + 64 + number
To South Africa: 020 + 27 + number

**Directory information service** 150
**Business and tourist information** 152

Postal services are generally good; there are post offices in all main towns and most major resorts, and there is a branch at the airport. The main post office in Port Louis is in Victoria Square (Ⓣ 208 2434). It costs R15 to send a 5-g airmail letter to Europe and southeast Asia, R17 to Australia, New Zealand, the USA and Canada and R14 to send a postcard anywhere in the world. Your hotel receptionist will normally sell you stamps and post your letters, but if in doubt always get your mail officially weighed at the post office and use the postboxes there rather than those found outside some shops. Postboxes at post offices are simple yellow boxes marked 'Inland' or 'Overseas', although to confuse matters you may see the latter in French as *Étranger*.

Internet and Wi-Fi access are available at most top hotels and there are Internet cafés in Port Louis, Grand Baie, Pereybère, Belle Mare and Flic en Flac.

## CUSTOMS

The Mauritian people are warm, welcoming and genuinely happy to meet visitors, not just from Europe, but from all over the world. Being such a multicultural nation with so many religions, they respond positively to what can locally be regarded as quirky Western ways.

You rarely come across displays of drunkenness in public places although you should watch out for drunk drivers on the roads, particularly at night. While the everyday language is Creole, most people working in tourism speak English and/or French and many switch effortlessly from one to another. What's more, if you learn a few words or phrases in Creole they'll appreciate the fact that you've tried.

The lifestyle may appear to be laid-back but many Mauritians work very hard so when a public holiday comes along – and there are many – no matter what religion they are, they all take the day off. This shouldn't affect hotel guests, but if planning to do anything special check that it's not a public holiday.

If invited to a Mauritian home it's quite acceptable to bring a small gift, such as flowers or sweets for the children. Expect lots of kissing on both cheeks among females but if you're a man the custom is simply to shake hands. Just go with it and enjoy!

## DRESS CODES

The emphasis is on smart-casual dress, particularly if you're staying in a top-end hotel. Skimpy beachwear is best left for the beach and after dark men are expected to wear long trousers for dinner. Light cotton dresses, shorts and tops are fine for the day and if visiting the capital. Topless sunbathing is not the done thing around hotel pools and is definitely a no-no on public beaches. If visiting a temple you should remove your shoes and cover up bare shoulders.

## ELECTRICITY

The power supply is 220 V. In hotels you'll come across power outlets designed for UK three-pin square plugs, French two-pin round plugs and South African three-pin round plugs. Hotels provide adaptors for foreign appliances but to be on the safe side pack your own and a torch for those occasions when you might be walking along unlit roads at night. Power cuts can and do happen but hotels have their own generators.

## EMERGENCIES

**Police** 999 **Fire** 995
**SAMU** (ambulance) 114
**Tourist Police** 210 3894

Private doctors and dentists are listed in the telephone directory or your hotel can make the necessary arrangements. Private medical care is mostly cheaper than in Europe and the standard of treatment is good.

### Private clinics

**Apollo Bramwell Hospital** Moka 605 1000
**Centre Medical du Nord** Pointe aux Canonniers 263 1010
**Clinique Darné** Floréal 601 2300
**Clinique du Nord** Tombeau Bay 247 2532
**Grand Baie Medical and Diagnostic Centre** Sottise Road 263 1212

### Public hospitals

**Doctor Jeetoo Hospital** Port Louis 212 3201
**Jawaharlal Nehru Hospital** Rose Belle 603 7000
**Princess Margaret Hospital** Quatre Bornes 425 3031
**SSR Hospital** Pamplemousses 243 3661

### Embassies & consulates

If you need legal representation contact your diplomatic representative.
**Australian High Commission** 2nd floor, Rogers House, President John Kennedy Street, Port Louis (230) 202 0160

**British High Commission** @ 7th floor, Les Cascades Building, Edith Cavell Street, Port Louis ① (248) 202 9400 ⓦ www.ukinmauritius.fco.gov.uk
**Canada High Commission** @ c/o Blanche Birger Company Ltd, 18 Jules Koenig Street ① (230) 212 5500
**New Zealand Consulate** @ Anchor Building, Anse Courtois Street, Les Pailles, Belle Village ① (230) 286 4920
**South African High Commission** @ 4th floor, BAI Building, Pope Hennessy Street, Port Louis ① (230) 212 6925
**United States Consulate** @ 4th floor, Rogers House, President John Kennedy Street, Port Louis ① (230) 202 4400 ⓦ http://mauritius. usembassy.gov

> ### SHARP STINGS
> Stings by marine life are rare but watch out for the venomous lion-, scorpion- and stonefish. Known as *laffe* in Creole, they inhabit rocky areas and muddy waters. If stung, seek medical help immediately. Many hotels and all hospitals stock the antidote.

## GETTING AROUND
### Driving rules & conditions
Mauritius has one of the highest road-death tolls in the world. Traffic moves dangerously slow or dangerously fast and you will often come across careless disregard for the Highway Code. Roads are generally in good condition but due to the absence of clear signposts, street lighting and proper pavements you should take care, especially at night, of speeding lorries and buses, pedestrians, stray dogs, unlit bicycles and drunk driving. Drive on the left-hand side of the road, always give heavy vehicles a wide berth and keep to the speed limits.

The speed limit is 40 kph (25 mph) in towns and villages, 60 kph (37 mph) elsewhere and 90 kph (56 mph) along the motorway linking the airport with the north. Drivers and all passengers must wear seat belts and children under ten must ride in the back. Avoid driving into Port Louis during the rush hours between 07.00–10.00 and 15.00–17.00

when roads can get very congested. If you must park in the capital you will need to display a parking coupon, available at most shops and petrol stations.

Always carry your driving licence with you. Remember that drinking and driving or using your mobile phone at the wheel carry heavy penalties.

## Car hire

Car hire starts from around R1,500 a day but do check that this includes insurance and taxes. Child safety seats are available from car hirers. To hire a car you must be over 21 and produce a valid international licence or an EU driving licence. Should you have an accident inform the hirer immediately. For 'damage only' accidents you need to complete an Agreed Statement of Facts form, which is provided by the hire company with your car.

### Car-hire companies

**Avis** ⓐ Port Louis ① 405 5200 Ⓦ www.avismauritius.com
**Budget Rent A Car** ⓐ Rose Hill ① 467 9700 Ⓦ www.mauritours.net
**Grand Baie Travel and Tours** ⓐ Coast Road, Trou aux Biches ① 265 5261
Ⓦ www.gbtt.com
**Monalysa Holidays Car Rental** ⓐ Grand Baie ① 728 6279
Ⓦ www.monalysatours.net

## Public transport

**By bus** Individual operators and co-operative societies run bus services to all parts of the island. Timetables are available at bus stations but in practice you won't need them as buses come along very regularly. Queues are usually orderly and it helps to tender the exact fare. Buses operate from 06.30–18.30 in the resorts and from 05.30–20.00 elsewhere and can get very crowded during rush hour. They're not ideal if travelling with very young children or if you are disabled since journeys can be slow or lightning fast depending on the whims of the driver. Accidents are common, particularly on narrow roads.

Fares range between R20 and R100 depending on the length of your journey, perhaps a little higher if you travel by air-conditioned express bus.

**By sea** The MS *Mauritius Pride* and MS *Mauritius Trochetia* sail to Rodrigues twice a month. The voyage takes 36 hours and you can book a cabin or travel in an air-conditioned seat. For a sailing schedule contact **MSC Coralline Ship Agency** (🅰 Nova Building, Military Road, Port Louis 🕿 217 2285 🆆 www.mauritiusshipping.intnet.mu).

**By air** Air Mauritius operates regular flights to Rodrigues. Seats fill quickly so book well in advance for the 90-minute flight. A recommended travel agent that can also organise flights and accommodation is **Concorde Travel** (🅰 Medine Mews, La Chausée, Port Louis 🕿 213 5280 🆆 www.concorde.mu 🅴 concordecpe@intnet.mu).

**Air Mauritius Helicopter Services** undertake airport transfers and scenic flights. The tariff for four people taking a 30-minute scenic flight or a direct transfer from the airport to your hotel for at least two people costs around R18,000. Contact your rep or Air Mauritius Helicopter Services (🕿 603 3754 🆆 www.airmauritius.com/helicopter.htm 🅴 helicopter@airmauritius.com).

## HEALTH, SAFETY & CRIME

You'll find standards of hygiene in luxury hotels and top-end restaurants on a par with Western standards and provided you take the same sensible precautions as you would at home you should not suffer any serious mishap. To avoid heat exhaustion, sunstroke and stomach upsets avoid staying out too long in the sun, wear a high-factor sunblock, drink plenty of water and make sure that fresh fruit and vegetables are washed before eating. Avoid empty restaurants and cold, uncovered food from street stalls and mobile food wagons. Tap water is safe to drink and bottled mineral water is widely available.

All doctors speak English and/or French and many have trained and practised abroad. Medical treatment is no longer free at government

**EXTREME SPORTS**

If embarking on any extreme sports, such as rock climbing, abseiling or quad biking do make sure that the operator is licensed and your guide is a qualified first aider. Check that emergency procedures are in place to deal with accidents or sudden illnesses. If you are in any doubt at all then don't book.

hospitals, but they are crowded and understaffed so you may have to join a long queue. In practice, visitors normally consult a private doctor and your hotel can arrange this for you. Expect to pay around R800 for a consultation. Generic drugs, which may appear under a different name, are available from pharmacies in resorts and towns throughout the island.

Most Mauritians are honest and helpful and levels of crime are low compared with other African countries. Any crime that does take place tends to be opportunistic so use caution as you would at home. Don't leave valuables unattended, particularly on the beach or in your car, lock all windows and doors of your accommodation and use the hotel safe. Sadly motorists have been robbed on the approach roads into and out of Port Louis so it's a good idea to lock your car doors from the inside.

Tourist police officers in Grand Baie work alongside the regular police force and you'll find most officers are polite and helpful; all of them speak English. Police officers wear open-necked light blue half-sleeve shirts, dark blue trousers and a flat hat with a chequered band.

## MEDIA

*News On Sunday* and *The Independent* are the only two locally produced English-language papers, while *News Now* (Ⓦ www.newsnow.mu) publishes online. *L'Express* (Ⓦ www.lexpress.mu) and *Le Matinal* (Ⓦ www.lematinal.com) are among the many French-language newspapers but they do contain some articles in English. Imported British newspapers, like the *Sunday Times* or the *Sunday Express*, are available in the larger supermarkets but they come at a price and are often a few days late. Look out for the free monthly English-language magazine called *Mauritius Info* (Ⓦ www.islandinfo.mu), which is packed with tourist information.

Mauritius Broadcasting Corporation (MBC) broadcasts news in English, French and Creole and there are several private radio stations, along with the ubiquitous satellite channels.

## OPENING HOURS

Post offices are open 08.15–16.00 Mon–Fri and 08.00–11.45 Sat.
Shops are normally open 09.00–17.00 Mon–Fri and 09.00–12.00 Sat.
Opening hours at petrol stations vary wildly but generally they are open 06.00–18.00 Mon–Sat and some are open for a few hours on Sunday.
Banks are open 09.00–15.30 Mon–Thur and 09.00–16.00 Fri. Banks at the airport are usually open for incoming flights.
Port Louis Market is open 06.00–18.00 Mon–Sat and 06.00–12.00 Sun.
Most restaurants and tourist attractions are closed on religious and public holidays so check before setting out.

## RELIGION

The diversity of religious beliefs in Mauritius is shown in the variety of festivals celebrated throughout the year. Of the population, 52 per cent practise Hinduism, 28 per cent Christianity (the majority of whom are Roman Catholic) and 16.5 per cent Islam. Many others practise Buddhism and a host of less familiar religions.

## SMOKING LAWS

A smoking ban is now in place, prohibiting smoking in all public places and buildings, including bars, cafés, restaurants, nightclubs, bus stops and stations, hospital grounds and public gardens. It is also banned on public transport (including taxis) and it is even prohibited in your own car if you are carrying passengers.

## TIME DIFFERENCES

Mauritius is four hours ahead of GMT, three hours ahead of British Summer Time and two hours ahead of European Summer Time. When it is noon in Mauritius it is 08.00 in London, 03.00 in New York, 20.00 in Sydney, 21.00 in Wellington.

## TIPPING

Most charges in restaurants and hotels include a 5–10 per cent service charge, so tipping is not obligatory. Taxi drivers and hotel staff do not expect tips but if you've had good service a nominal tip, of say 5 per cent, is always warmly received.

## TOILETS

Public toilets in attractions and shopping malls and on most beaches are free and clean. They are normally equipped with toilet paper, washbasins and hand dryers. There are free public toilets on the Caudan Waterfront in Port Louis, but avoid those in markets and bus stations. Cafés and restaurants will normally let you use their toilet if you need one urgently.

## TRAVELLERS WITH DISABILITIES

Special assistance and wheelchairs are available at the airport but facilities at hotels vary. Most hotels are low-rise, some have specially equipped rooms and others occupy flat and spacious grounds.
Before making a firm booking, check with your travel agent or direct with the hotel to confirm what facilities are available. Two useful websites for travellers with disabilities are Ⓦ www.makoa.org/travel and Ⓦ www.disabilitytravel.co.uk

## ACKNOWLEDGEMENTS

Thomas Cook Publishing wishes to thank ERIC ROBERTS, to whom the copyright belongs, for the photographs in this book, except for the following images:

PCL TRAVEL pages 37 (Geraint Tellem), 42 (Stuart Black), 59 (Yann Gulchaoua); WIKIMEDIA COMMONS page 34 (Alexey M).

For CAMBRIDGE PUBLISHING MANAGEMENT LIMITED:
Project editor: Tom Lee
Layout: Trevor Double
Proofreaders: Rosalind Munro & Cath Senker
Indexer: Marie Lorimer

### Send your thoughts to
# books@thomascook.com

- Found a beach bar, peaceful stretch of sand or must-see sight that we don't feature?
- Like to tip us off about any information that needs a little updating?
- Want to tell us what you love about this handy, little guidebook and, more importantly, how we can make it even handier?

Then here's your chance to tell all! Send us ideas, discoveries and recommendations today and then look out for your valuable input in the next edition of this title.

Email to the above address or write to:
pocket guides Series Editor, Thomas Cook Publishing, PO Box 227, Unit 9, Coningsby Road, Peterborough PE3 8SB, UK.